FREE IN CHRIST

CECIL HOOK

Order from:

CECIL and LEA HOOK
1350 Huisache
New Braunfels, Tex
(512) 625-16

D1219763

Comp
cc

CONTENTS:

Author's Preface

Unless you make Rip Van Winkle appear to be an early riser by comparison, you are aware that our religious world is in an exciting state of reform. You may not be too aware, however, that the Church of Christ is in a time of re-evaluation also. We should have led in reform, but our changes have been made with much reluctance and they continue to meet rigid resistance.

This is a message of reappraisal, correction, and reform. Those both in and out of the Church of Christ may be pleased to learn that there is some recognition of our misdirection and that sincere effort is being made to correct it. If, however, you are frightened, shaken, or agitated by the suggestion that we in the Churches of Christ may not have all the neat answers as we have supposed, this book is not for you. It is for you who are still asking questions, searching, and trying to be disciples in the fuller sense of life-long learners.

It requires a great deal of audacity to assume the role of teacher and corrector of others, especially when the would-be instructor has no more academic qualification than I. Please do not let my foolhardiness turn you off. I am willing to make myself vulnerable in this effort to spare other sincere searchers some of the agony that I have experienced in my long effort to reconcile our simplistic orthodox interpretations with the Scriptures. I depended upon learning "here a little, there a little" in fitting the puzzling picture together, but I have the high ambition of making this a sort of course of indoctrination to lead one from our divisive, legalistic, and exclusivist doctrinal centered religion into the exciting acceptance and freedom in Christ. Maybe I am not out of the woods altogether yet, but I have gained enough of the freedom in Christ to know that it is worth sharing.

My message is intended for the pew people rather than the scholars. I respect scholarship but claim none for myself. And

I am intimidated and sensitive concerning originality. I have had very poor study habits. Throughout my ministry, none of my lessons were ever written out before delivery. So I have not kept footnotes and proper credits for points learned from others. Thoughts of others have become a part of my thinking. That is a part of learning, whether it be ideas received from Early Arceneaux, Charles H. Roberson, or Homer Hailey in my youth, or from Wes Reagan, Carl Ketcherside, or Leroy Garrett in more recent years. Since the last three have been on the cutting edge of reform, I give them much credit for influencing my thinking. So, if any point made in this material seems to be taken from them or anyone else, I plead guilty with no contest. I offer this as an explanation, not as an excuse.

God has worked in numerous ways recently to convince me that He wants this to be my ministry in my time of retirement from congregational ministry. Private study groups have discussed these essays and numerous preachers have read them. These have given me strong encouragement to publish them. They have convinced me that the time is ripe for this book. Your feedback is encouraged.

God has worked to combine our ministry with that of two other families whom He has endowed with the beautiful gift of giving. In response to the Spirit rather than to any request or hint of mine, a New Braunfels disciple called to say that he and his family wanted to finance the printing of my manuscript which they had just finished reading. They desire no personal recognition for it. They only want you to share what they have felt and to give God the praise.

God is working through a Dallas couple also who called to say that they want to bear the mailing costs in distributing the books. What a blessing to us and to you! These all are truly unselfish in giving you the book without cost to you. God knows who they are and He will reward their self-denial.

Upon my full retirement after ten years of ministry with the church here, the congregation gave my wife, Lea, and me a life estate of the residence here. How blessed we are! So this will be our address until the Lord sees fit to make us change. We have little retirement other than Social Security, so we contracted the janitorial work of the church as a supplement. Yes, this book is the work of a janitor! (I also give you good straight lines!) Lea shares as an equal partner in all of our life's work together and in what good or ill may come from this writing. We invite you to share in our ministry by helping to put it into the hands of persons who long for unity, acceptance, and freedom in Christ.

May we share the glorious freedom that is in Christ both now and forever.

Cecil Hook

October 1, 1984

Preface to the Fourth Printing

When we anxiously published this little volume, we could hardly have dreamed that it would enjoy such a wide reception. The Lord has directed it to open hearts throughout the nation and in many other countries. We praise him for that.

In the third printing we dropped the original plan of free distribution in favor of retailing the books. Readers have been kind to purchase them, thus helping our personal financial situation in our retirement. However, unsolicited donations have continued to come, mostly from persons whom we have never known. We thank God for these partners in this ministry of freedom and we feel deeply the trust that they have placed in us.

As long as such funds make it possible, we will continue to supply free copies to those who wish to pass them on to others but cannot afford to do it. Even without such funds, Lea and I hope always to be able to give free copies to students, preacher trainees, missionaries, and others who cannot afford to buy them. We consider this a ministry, not a business; we want the message to go out. So, ask for the books. We still depend upon person-to-person advertisement. Thanking you for your help in that, we encourage you to continue.

Even though she looks much too young for it, Lea now draws her Social Security enabling us to give up our janitorial work!

Your many calls, letters, visits, and prayers have been a soul-lifting encouragement to us. God bless you for them. Please continue!

Cecil Hook

May 18, 1988

Chapter I

THE ISSUES BEFORE US

We are divided! While we in the Church of Christ have plead fervently for unity, we have continued to divide. The very message which we proclaim in hopes of creating unity has been the cause of division by its nature.

The splintered, sectarian divisions claim to be the one true church. Those on the left often look condescendingly upon those on the right while those on the right condemn those on the left. Both those on the left and the right usually set themselves against all who do not denominate (name) themselves "Church of Christ."

A special reasoning has developed which produces and defends this lamentable condition. It begins with a legal approach to the Scriptures and justification. According to this line of thinking, since salvation depends upon rightly keeping of law, each point of the law must be known and practiced in detail. There is no room for difference of understanding or practice. Unity and fellowship are based upon total doctrinal agreement, ruling out any thought of unity in diversity. This mentality will continue to emphasize differences and force those distinctions into dividing issues.

A person has only to sit in one of our Bible class discussions to see how foolish our claim for doctrinal unity is. No two of us agree on everything. We cannot evade this point. To emphasize this point, a list of one hundred issues over which individuals have disagreed is given below. We have continued in congregational fellowship while disagreeing on these many points; thus our very practice has been inconsistent with our denial of unity in diversity.

1. taking of oaths
2. serving in the military

3. inflicting capital punishment
4. using force to defend one's self or others
5. voting for political candidates
6. serving as a governmental official
7. engaging in political activism
8. playing cards
9. calling on a member of "a division" to lead prayer
10. permitting an unbaptized boy to lead singing at any service
11. joining a ministerial alliance
12. indwelling of the Holy Spirit
13. work of the Holy Spirit
14. baptism of the Holy Spirit
15. praying for healing
16. the Trinity
17. special providence
18. how God answers prayer
19. fasting
20. translations of the Bible
21. use of "Thee" and "Thou" in prayer
22. authority of elders
23. who selects and appoints elders
24. qualifications of elders
25. tenure of elders
26. elders presiding at the Lord's Table
27. qualifications of deacons
28. deaconnesses
29. enrolling widows
30. addressing disciples with military/academic titles: "Major" or "Doctor"
31. long hair on men; women with short hair worshipping unveiled
32. midweek contributions
33. dimming the lights during prayer
34. singing as the emblems and collection baskets are passed
35. use of church buildings for secular activities like Boy Scout meetings

36. use of pictures of Jesus
37. use of symbols such as the cross
38. use of steeples and stained glass windows
39. use of the term "Sunday School" rather than "Bible classes"
40. passing of the collection baskets
41. eating in the church building
42. grounds for disfellowshipping
43. support of colleges from the church treasury
44. divorce for any cause
45. remarriage of a divorced person
46. preacher officiating at a wedding of a divorced person
47. disciples marrying non-members
48. preacher officiating at the wedding of a member and a non-member
49. use of an instrument in the church building for weddings
50. method and type of inspiration of the Bible
51. re-baptism of Baptists and Christian Church members
52. the "five items of worship"
53. use of choirs, choruses, quartets, solos, etc.
54. serving the Lord's Supper on Sunday evening
55. serving the Lord's Supper at family reunions, camp-outs, etc.
56. integration of races
57. smoking
58. total abstinence from alcoholic beverages
59. membership in fraternal orders
60. contributing to such as the United Fund or Community Chest
61. use of Bible class literature
62. youth directors, youth rallies, youth camps
63. the six days of creation being literal days
64. the extent of evolution
65. the operation of Christian hospitals
66. awards and prizes for church activities
67. debating religious issues
68. ministers of education, ministers of music etc.

69. benevolence to fellow-disciples only
70. the baptismal "formula"
71. formal confession before baptism
72. going to law against disciples
73. slavery
74. signing contribution pledge cards
75. children's homes under eldership or a board
76. dancing
77. women wearing shorts and slacks
78. women wearing slacks to church services
79. girls leading prayer in family devotionals
80. girls leading prayer in youth devotionals
81. "the plan" versus "the Man"
82. buying VBS refreshments from the treasury
83. present day activity of demons
84. the local church obeying each command given to individuals
85. use of God's name as a by-word
86. use of euphemisms of God's name in by-words and expletives
87. use of contraceptives
88. abortion
89. adopting out an illegitimate child
90. women working outside the home
91. Children's Bible Hour
92. bussing children to services
93. "What is to be will be."
94. bodily resurrection
95. if we shall know each other in heaven
96. degrees of reward and punishment
97. whether heaven and hell are literal places
98. dress code for men serving the Lord's Supper
99. offering thanks for the contribution
100. a name for the church

No doubt, you can add to this rounded list of 100 issues. This listing borrows heavily from a list by Patrick M. Phillips, who also gives credit to James Robert Jarrell, in Mission Messenger, May 1971. How absurd it is for us to pretend to be united doctrinally when it is not likely that there is even one small congregation among us that is in total agreement on all these matters.

Then there are the "big" issues over which we have created open division, aligning brethren in different sectarian, exclusive groups. Phillips noted thirty divisions due to doctrinal distinctions. I have known of divisions based on the following doctrinal distinctions and practical issues:

1. use of Sunday School classes
2. use of women teachers
3. use of multiple communion cups
4. premillenialism
5. congregations cooperating in evangelism through a sponsoring church
6. supporting Christian orphanages from the local treasury
7. speaking in tongues
8. cooking and eating in the church building
9. the "located minister" system
10. the use of instrumental music in worship
11. the use of missionary, benevolent, and other types of societies or organizations to carry out Christian activities

In developing such issues we have become hair-splitters serving a God of quibbles. Sincerely, but being either ignorant or intellectually dishonest, we have twisted and misapplied Scriptures to support our contentions. We have become fixed in the tracks of dogmatism. God's purposes in His directives have been overshadowed by emphasis on lawful requirements. Binding incidental details often becomes more important than the love without which we cannot be bound together. Doctrine, instead of the Savior, has become our center. The binding of scruples has limited the liberties of others. We do not trust others with the freedom which Christ gives. We have become judgmental and exclusive and have given ourselves a name to distinguish us from others. God's grace has been limited to our achievement. We continue not only to divide but also to prevent the only true unity. Unless we change our perspective, we shall continue on this ill-fated course.

As the forty-plus years of my ministry passed and I continued to learn, it became evident to me that we were in need of much correction of course. Our group philosophy and attitude, however, allowed for little correction. We were right in all the things that counted! I learned that all the truth is not permitted from our pulpits. When the financial security of the preacher's family is threatened by each new thought that he introduces, it is easy for him to rationalize that it is better to wait. But how long must we wait? Years have fled by and my time of opportunity on earth is limited. Shall I wait for another generation to speak out when I lacked the courage to do so? Shall we allow our misdirection to be perpetuated? Some have led the way courageously. I, too, must speak out! I want to do what I can to correct the course of those whom I spent my years sincerely misdirecting. I hope that I am ready to pay the cost.

Although this is my lover's quarrel with the people I hold dear, it is not a negative and bitter assault on them. There are positive solutions. So, stay with me through the chapters ahead, and may God bless you and me through this study together.

Chapter 2

Law and Principle

Why do we have so many commands and directives from God? Does He have some kind of divinely selfish interest that is fulfilled by His burdening us with requirements and restrictions? Does He have an ego problem which would cause Him to demand, "You people on earth, I command you to sing praises to me"?

The legislators of Texas passed a law that each automobile licensed in the state must have an inspection sticker on the driver's side of the windshield. They made that law because some of us are careless about keeping our cars in safe operating condition. The law is for the good of the owner of the car and for the others who might be jeopardized by its operation. So the law is for the good of all concerned.

Suppose that our legislators should pass another law requiring a green star sticker on the passenger side of the windshield. They explain the purpose of this law: "We made this law just to let you know that we have the authority to legislate. We want you to get this sticker simply because we say for you to get it." That would be an arbitrary, despotic law. And after the next election there would be some new faces in the legislature!

Law must originate from authority in order to have validity; yet just laws are not arbitrary expressions of authority.

Laws are designed for the benefit and protection of the governed. Each law is based upon some good or moral principle. A command without a principle is arbitrary, only satisfying a despotic whim.

God's laws are not arbitrary expressions of authority. His commands are not for the satisfying of the whims of an egocentric deity. His laws are based upon the principle of what is good for man and just with God. A command expediting a principle may contain some element of arbitrary choice like God's choice of the seventh day as the sabbath. Commands only direct and expedite the application of the principles involved. Rather than initiating rituals of sacramental value, God's commands direct man in the receiving of grace and growing in grace in the spiritual realm and in the living responsibly with his fellow man in the moral realm.

The principle is broader and greater than the command. Man's tendency has been to emphasize the lawful demand and to minimize or fail to discern the principle. This is a facet of legalism.

The Ten Commandments, for instance, were not arbitrary laws, but were based on principles even though the Jews interpreted them as being arbitrary. In the first three God is saying, "I love you and want your full fellowship." In the fifth through the tenth, He is saying, "Love and respect each other." The fourth command, "Remember the sabbath day to keep it holy," might seem not to fit with the nine. However, it is the pivotal command. It points both directions — to God and man. In it God is saying, "Remember your spiritual relationship with me and remember the dignity and purpose of man."

The Jews accepted the sabbath command as a most absolute and arbitrary expression of God's will. They sought to define all the legalities relating to this commmand while minimizing or failing to discern the principles it was designed to promote.

Law in Perspective

One man defied God and was put to death for gathering firewood on the sabbath (Num. 15:32-36). But Jesus put the law in true perspective. He considered mercy shown to a sheep to be more important than the sabbath law (Matt. 12:9-12). He also explained, "The sabbath was made for man, not man for the sabbath" (Mk. 2:27). Law was made for the benefit of man. Man was not made to comply with arbitrary law.

There are two levels of responsibility. One person passes a school with reduced speed and great caution because of concern for innocent children. Another person speeds by with no concern. For this person, a sign must be posted which defines fifteen miles per hour as the speed limit and a policeman must be around to help enforce it. Since this man does not accept responsibility out of concern, he must be forced to accept it by law. Paul explained that "the law is not laid down for the just but for the lawless and disobedient . . ." (1Tim. 1:8). The first person needed no law. Law was made for the second.

There are two levels of obedience. A man has two sons who go out on their dates. To each he says, "Come home early; please don't stay out late." The more mature son realizes that his father and mother won't sleep a wink until he comes home and that he himself must go to school the next morning. So he comes home at a very reasonable hour. The less mature son comes in at two o'clock. When confronted about it, he exclaims, "Dad, you did not say how late late is and how early early is!" For this son the father must make a rigid law: Ten o'clock or you will be punished! One son is guided by principles; the other is guided by legal specifications.

We see both levels of responsibility and obedience in God's family. Our immaturity has been evident. We often search earth and heaven to find all the legal requirements and limitations. We discuss, wrangle, debate, judge, and censor to the point of alienating and dividing while missing the principle that God had in mind. Often where authoritative specifications have been lacking, we have formulated our own by specious logic. And, in case all else fails, we have devised elder authority to define and bind lawful specifications. That is the ultimate of legalism. Such an approach will keep us confused, enslaved, and divided.

Jesus spoke out against those who sought justification by keeping legal requirements. The scribes and Pharisees were so scrupulous about keeping the law of the tithe that they would not overlook the sprigs of seasoning herbs in their gardens — mint, rue, and dill (Matt. 23:23; Lk. 11:42). God's directive concerning tithing was not given because He had need of food or money nor because God wanted to lay a burden on man to test him. God wanted this to be given for the welfare of His people. The Pharisees were looking for specifics as to how to keep the technicality of the law when they should have been using what they had to promote love, mercy, justice, and faith which the tithe was meant to promote. They were seeking to be justified by keeping law when they should have been seeking to accomplish its purposes.

We should not perform just to obey commands, but also for the value to be received from what was commanded. It is truly a trust in legal justification that causes a person to obey commands simply because they are commands. The person who has mercy, justice, faith, and love as his concern fulfills the principle and does not need a law to tell him how much of his resources to use in accomplishing these. He is free from lawful requirements because he has the principle written on his heart.

God wants us to gather for mutual edification (1 Cor. 14:26). In assemblies we pray for each other, teach each other, teach and admonish one another in singing, give to help each other, and proclaim the atonement to each other. But in too many cases the thing stressed is the importance of assembling in response to a command rather than fulfilling the purposes God had in mind. To make the lawful case stronger, appeal is made to elder authority to lawfully specify the time of assembly. Providing uplifting services will more nearly fulfill the purpose than demanding attendance.

Not Many Commands

Really, there are not a great many authoritative commands directed to us. We are directed into action in at least these seven ways: (1) explicit order, (2) entreaty, (3) exhortation, (4) rehetorical questions, (5) statements of personal acceptance, (6) statement of conditions, and (7) advice of expediency. None of these bind a condition or restriction on us unless they foster some principle for the benefit of man which is expedited by the statement or instruction.

There are many directives given in the New Testament. Surely, we do not follow them all. How may we judge which ones are demands upon us? It is not always easy to judge, so we must not be too dogmatic. We must look for principles. It is not imperative for us unless the teaching or command is directing the accomplishing of a practical purpose.

This all leads us to a striking and exciting conclusion: It is the principle that should rule our conduct rather than the command. A "command" promoting no principle is not really a command. The immature in perception may still prefer the command approach, seeking legal specifications. But the more mature will be seeking to accomplish the good fostered by the directive rather than trying to gain a score of righteousness by keeping the technicality of the law. The difference in approach will determine whether we gain the approval or denunciation of our Savior.

Since many sincere interpreters contend that incidental historical details, which we have considered as examples, have the same authority that commands and laws have, it is appropriate here to ask which examples are binding.

Which of these nine examples of details concerning the Lord's Supper are binding? It was eaten (1) at night, (2) upstairs, (3) in midweek, (4) during another meal, (5) with no women present, and there was (6) one loaf, (7) of unleavened bread and, (8) one cup, (9) of Passover wine which could not have been fresh grape juice at that season. Which exemplified detail is binding?

Incidental Details

No examples are binding!

An example shows how a command may be obeyed or how a principle may be fulfilled, but an example does not necessarily illustrate the only way. The authoritative quality is in the command, not in the example. For instance, Philip's immersing the eunuch is not a binding example of immersion. It only exemplifies the meaning of *baptizo*, the Greek word used in the command to baptize.

There are many actions recorded that are not binding examples because they illustrate no command or principle. Philip's running to the chariot is not bound on us as an example of how to fulfill the "go" of the Great Comission. Those who bind examples are very selective in the examples they choose to bind.

All that we have been covering in this lesson can be illustrated very well in regard to the Lord's Supper. Jesus said, "Do this in remembrance of me." This is no arbitrary command. It has a purpose. The purpose is not to flatter Jesus or to take a census of the faithful. It is to keep the atonement, the basis of our hope, ever fresh in our minds. We eat it, not to fulfill a command, or for a sacramental grace that it might impart, but to strengthen and express our faith in the atonement. In so doing, we show forth His death till He comes and we discern the oneness of the body.

If its purpose is to make us think on the atonement, then what difference does it make at what hour or on what day we do it, or if we do it twice on a day or several times weekly? What is the concern about whether the cup be fresh or fermented, or whether the bread be leavened or unleavened? How could sequence be of importance — whether we break the bread before or after the prayer, whether the bread be taken before the cup, or whether they both be served at the same time? Such details have nothing to do with the purpose of participation. If a person derives the benefit of this remembrance on Wednesday instead of Sunday, does it suddenly become a curse instead of a blessing?

Many prayers at the Lord's Table include: "May we partake of it in the way that is acceptable and pleasing in Thy sight." What do we mean by that? I think that generally we mean that Jesus commanded a lawful procedure of the right elements to be taken in the right order on the right day with the right people, etc., and our prayer is that we have not slipped up on any technicality so as to eat and drink damnation to our souls. Such expresses an effort to fulfill legal requirements by obeying commands rather than to fulfull the purpose of refreshing our memories.

"But we are commanded to break bread on the first day of the week," we hear someone protest. Where is that command? Jesus could have made such a stipulation very easily, but He did not! It took our legalistic logic to come up with that command. Surely, we are not left to piece together vague clues to build up our case on such an important matter.

But what about Troas? It says, "On the first day of the week, when we were gathered together to break bread . . . " (Acts 20:7f). First, we assume that this breaking of bread is the Communion rather than a love feast or fellowship meal. Although there is no proof of it, we will grant that it was the Communion for argument's sake. Assuming that they met to commune, it does not indicate that they had been doing so previously or that they continued to do so the next week and thereafter. There is no indication that this was done except on that one particular weekend. This is the only time the breaking of bread is mentioned in connection with the first day of the week!

There is no clear example of the Lord's Supper ever being eaten on the first day of the week. At Troas, if they met according to Roman (and our) manner of reckoning time, they met to eat it on our Sunday night but did not partake until Monday morning because of Paul's long discourse. If they followed the Jewish calendar, they met to partake of it on our Saturday night. Would we be right in participating on Saturday night or Monday morning? If we were trying to be righteous by keeping legal specifications, this would be a vital matter. If we wish to accomplish the purpose of the Communion, these details fade into insignificance. We do not commune to obey commands and follow examples but to remember that Jesus died for our sins.

Not Nit-Picking

I know that I am attacking sacred cows. Please do not judge me to be irreverent. I am exposing our intellectually dishonest use of fallacious argument to support claims to legal righteousness. All of our traditional procedures have not been based on commands which expedite principles or on examples based on commands.

This is not just nit-picking. Sincere Pharisees were eager to keep the commandment to tithe in its most minute details. They gained a sense of rightness through it, but they missed the purpose of the tithe commandment. The purpose was to promote justice, mercy, faith, and love. This exercise, rather than just obeying the command to tithe, was what God wanted. Jesus pronounced a woe upon them for their misdirected purpose. He will not be any more pleased with us than with them when we follow their pattern.

I have been a disciple for fifty years, being brought up in "the strictest sect of the Pharisees." I have taught all the old arguments for many years. My difficult struggle has been in facing the Scriptures honestly. I can sympathize truly with any who might be shocked by this discourse. Once the light begins to break through, however, many other points will take on new and richer meaning, and I can assure you that you will begin to breathe the fresh air of freedom in Christ.

Chapter 3

WHAT IS THE LAW OF CHRIST?

"Bear one another's burdens, and so fulfill the law of Christ" (Gal. 6:2). What is the law of Christ?

Jesus has assured us, "For the law was given through Moses; grace and truth came through Jesus Christ" (John 1:17). Paul told disciples, "For by grace you have been saved through faith; and this is not your own doing, it is the gift of God — not because of works, lest any man should boast" (Eph. 2:8f). The grace of God appeared, teaching us (Titus 2:11f). The gospel is the message of grace to be believed for salvation (Mark 16:15f). We are saved by grace; however, under Moses' law men had sought justification by law, and there is great tendency for disciples to seek righteousness through keeping of law also.

1. COULD ONE BE SAVED BY WORKS OF THE LAW? Paul gave a definite negative answer to this question. "For no human being will be justified in his sight by works of the law, since through the law comes the knowledge of sin" (Rom. 3:20). "By works of the law shall no one be justified" (Gal. 2:16). "I do not nullify the grace of God; for if justification were through the law, then Christ died for no purpose" Gal. 2:21). "Now it is evident that no man is justified before God by the law" (Gal. 3:11).

The law had a weakness: it could bring death, but not life. It made nothing perfect (Heb. 7:18f). It promised life but proved to be death (Rom. 7:10) because a person was required to keep all the law or be cursed (Gal. 3:10f), and none could keep it all. So all had the sentence of death.

That same weakness prevents any law from saving. Law has no power to save. John assures us that all of us sin (1 John 1:8f). James adds, "For whoever keeps the whole law but fails in one point has become guilty of all of it (James 2:10). If we keep 99% of the law, but fail in the remaining one percent, what happens? We are back to zero! So it is all by grace! If one is to be saved, it must be totally by grace. One cannot be saved partly by law keeping and partly by grace. If grace saves only to the extent that one is able to keep law, then none can be saved. If one could keep all the law, he would need no grace. Our traditional exhortation to the one who fails to keep all the law is: "Try harder!" While giving lip-service to grace, we frustrate disciples by urging that they must attain it by keeping all·the law — or making a passing score, whatever that may be. Claim of justification by law keeping was "another gospel" of Galatians 1:6-9. Any effort to be justified by legal means is a falling away from grace (Gal. 5:4). Grace is not a quality of law.

One legal system did not replace another. The law was given through Moses; grace and truth came through Jesus. Grace and truth were not a system of law to replace the old one. God did not send another law, but He sent His Son in whom we may be justified. To saved persons, Paul explained, "For sin will have no dominion over you, since you are not under law but under grace" (Rom. 6:14). Please read Romans 3:20-28 and observe that justification apart from law is by grace as a free gift to those who believe. Righteousness is not attained by rule keeping, but it is a free gift (Rom. 5:17). Also please read another passage of length, Galatians 3:23; 4:7, to learn that, now that faith has come, the custodian is no longer in charge and that God sent His Son instead of another legal custodian. Ours is a personal relationship in Him instead of a legal relationship.

2. WHAT IS THE NATURE OF OUR RELATIONSHIP TO GOD? The Spirit makes us new creatures in Christ. "But now we are discharged from the law, dead to that which held us captive, so that we serve not under the old written code but in the new life of the Spirit" (Rom. 7:6). This new relationship is accomplished through the new birth (John 3:3f), by which we are all sons of God through faith (Gal. 3:26f), and in which our life becomes hidden with Christ in God (Col. 3:3). It is not a legal relationship, but a spiritual one.

We enter into a covenant relationship. God made a covenant with Abraham and sealed it by circumcision (Gen 19:9f). Later the law was given to guide the covenant people (Deut. 4:4f).

The law was not the covenant of promise, nor did it make them covenant people.

The new covenant is sealed in us by the Holy Spirit (Eph. 1:13f). This is done when we receive the Spirit at the time of our obedience to the gospel; the other teachings are given to guide those in covenant relationship.

The new covenant is not a written code. Paul wrote that God "has qualified us to be ministers of a new covenant, not in a written code but in the Spirit; for the written code kills, but the Spirit gives life" (2 Cor. 3:6). Hebrews 8:7-8 further emphasizes that the new covenant would not be like the old one. His law is to be written on our hearts instead of stone or paper.

How can law be written on our hearts if we are not under law? To say that we are not under law is not to say that we are not under the lordship of Christ and the sovereignty of God. "Law" has a range of meanings. Law may be a legal system which demands perfect obedience. Law also can be a principle of action. We are justified through the principle of grace through faith (Eph. 2:8f; Rom. 3:27f; 8:1f). That grace activates our love.

3. WHAT IS THE NEW COVENANT RULE OF ACTION? It is love which God in His grace infuses into our hearts. "God's love has been poured into our hearts through the Holy Spirit which has been given to us" (Rom. 5:5). "We love, because he first loved us" (1 John 4:19). God initiates the principle of loving action, writing His law upon our hearts.

The love which He has created in us is the master key to unlock the servile chain of any other law. "Owe no man anything, except to love one another; for he who loves his neighbor has fulfilled the law. The commandments, 'You shall not commit adultery, You shall not kill, You shall not steal, You shall not covet,' and any other commandment, are summed up in this sentence, 'You shall love your neighbor as yourself.' Love does no wrong to a neighbor; therefore love is the fulfilling of the law" (Rom. 13:8f). Love fulfills God's requirements. It frees us. A legal code enslaves. "For freedom Christ has set us free; stand fast therefore, and do not submit again to a yoke of slavery" (Gal. 5:1).

Paul emphasizes these points again in Galatians 5:13f: "For

you were called to freedom, brethren; only do not use your freedom as an opportunity for the flesh, but through love be servants of one another. For the whole law is fulfilled in one word, 'You shall love your neighbor as yourself.' " What greater and more comprehensive law — principle of action — could we want? How would a listing of authoritative demands help a person show love?

God directs us into right relationship with Him and man. "And he said to him, 'You shall love the Lord your God with all your heart, and with all your soul, and with all your mind. This is the great and first commandment. And a second is like it, You shall love your neighbor as yourself. On these two commandments depend all the law and the prophets' " (Matt. 22:37f). All through the ages, God was trying to get us simply to love Him and one another. That was the purpose of the law and the message of the prophets. God has shown us how to express that love through commands, exhortations, teachings, principles, and examples. Man has tried consistently to interpret these as lawful requirements, but God gave them as directives to love. Men argue, fight, and divide over lawful interpretations and thereby defeat the love into which God was directing. "For in Christ Jesus neither circumcision nor uncircumcision (legal hair-splitting: CH) is of any avail, but faith working through love" (Gal. 5:6). As covenant people we are guided by these, but not justified by them. When we sin as disciples, we depend upon grace for our forgiveness rather than obeying more laws (1 John 1:5-10; 2:1-6).

Does this encourage sin, disobedience, and indifference? Anticipating such a question, Paul answers, "What shall we say then? Are we to continue in sin that grace may abound? By no means! How can we who died to sin still live in it?" (Rom. 6:1f). He warns against abuse of our freedom, then cautions, "But I say, walk by the Spirit, and do not gratify the desires of the flesh" (Gal. 5:13-16). Freedom is not for unrestrained indulgence.

4. WHAT IS THE LAW OF CHRIST? Some would contend that the entirety of the New Testament writings is the law of Christ. Then, is the account of the birth and temptation of Jesus

the law of Christ? What of the love chapter, the resurrection chapter, and Revelation? Are these all part of the law of Christ? The law of Christ is not a book, a listing, or a code of laws. Where is such a catalog of laws? The Jews enumerated 613 laws in their legal code. How many laws has Christ given us? Since we are to keep the law of Christ, surely someone has counted and listed those laws so we will have a check-list! Where is such a list?

Christ's law is love; yet He gives us commands, examples, exhortations, warnings, and principles as guidelines for the expression of love — our response to grace.

Christ's law is love. His laws (plural) are (1) love God, and (2) love man. Love is the new commandment (John 13:34f) which John's readers had heard from the beginning of their discipleship (1 John 2:7f). "And now I beg you, lady, not as though I were writing you a new commandment, but the one we have heard from the beginning, that we love one another. And this is love, that we follow his commandments; this is the commandment, as you have heard from the beginning, that you follow love" (2 John 5f).

"And this commandment we have from him, that he who loves God should love his brother also" (1 John 4:21) is a re-emphasis of the first and second commandments. Love is the royal, kingly law (James 2:8).

Expressed love fulfills the law of Christ (Gal. 6:2). Love is the perfect law, the law of liberty (James 1:25; 2:12) — liberty from an imperfect legal code and efforts for legal justification. It is the Golden Rule (Matt. 7:12), that ageless law which conveys the intent and message of the law and the prophets. '

How beautiful this is! God initiates the response of love: "We love, because he first loved us." He begins the working of His law in our hearts. He wants us to express it. His directives guide us in expressing it: "If you love me, you will keep my commandments" (John 14:15). So, our expressions of love become God's expressions of love through us, "For this is the love of God, that we keep his commandments, and his commandments are not burdensome" (1 John 5:3). No burden! "There is no fear in love, but perfect love casts out fear. For fear has to do with punishment, and he who fears is not perfected in love" (1 John 4:18). No fear! Keeping His law of love is neither fearful nor burdensome!

We are justified by grace through faith in obeying the gospel. Efforts to be justified by law would nullify the grace of Christ. Our response to God's grace is the love which God initiates in us. The New Testament writings guide our love into proper expression.

"Now therefore why do you make trial of God by putting a yoke upon the neck of the disciples which neither our fathers nor we have been able to bear?" (Actls 15:10).

Chapter 4

WHY IS LOVE THE GREAT COMMANDMENT?

It is refreshing that so much emphasis is now being given to Jesus' teaching about love. We all know that Jesus spoke of love for God as the great commandment and love for man as the second greatest (Matt. 22:34-40). But why is love the great commandment?

Love is the great commandment because (1) it is the only effective motivation for our actions, (2) it fulfills the intent of all other laws, (3) it lifts us above efforts of legal justification, and (4) it transcends any sense of duty. Let us consider each of these reasons.

1. Although love is commanded, it can hardly be instilled by command. A husband cannot gain or hold the love of his wife or children by command. If love is an action of the will in response to an authentic command, then it is a forced love. Compelled love is contrary to the nature of love. And if the greatest of commands cannot be fulfilled by demand, we may expect the same to be true relating to the lesser commands.

Love must be instilled. It comes in response to love rather than lawful demands. God "so loved the world" in order to create love in us. "God commends his own love toward us, in that, while we were yet sinners, Christ died for us" (Rom. 5:8). Jesus took the form of man and died for us to gain our loving response (Phil. 2:5-7; John 15:14). It is striking that John did not say, "We love because he first commanded us." He simply stated, "We love because he first loved us" (1 John 4:19). Likewise, Paul recognized the true motivating force in our lives as undeserved love, explaining that "the love of Christ constrains us" (2 Cor. 5:14).

There is a proper place for fear, but "There is no fear in love: but perfect love casts out fear" (1 John 4:18). The motivation of fear will make us ineffective, for "if I bestow all my goods to feed the poor, and if I give my body to be burned, but have not love, it profits me nothing" (1 Cor 13:3). No one will be scared into heaven. The fearful will have their place in the lake that burns with fire and brimstone (Rev. 21:8). Love is the great commandment because it is the only effective motivation for our discipleship.

2. Love is the fulfillment of the law. There are two kinds of relationships governed by two kinds of law. Spiritual laws regulate our relationship to God and moral laws guide our man-to-man relationships.

We would not know how to relate to God or how to serve Him if it were not revealed. Jesus said, "If you love me, you will keep my commandments" (John 14:15). God's directions tell us how to serve Him but do not define the extent of service. Our worship and service are expressions of love. One should not attend, pray, sing, give, etc. because he is commanded to do so. He should do these as an expression of loving relationship. The instructions only tell us how to express our love. Most of these directives are exhortations rather than lawful demands; hence, we are exhorted to attend, pray, sing, and give. We have been inclined to bind amounts required in our giving and assembling expecting God to enforce our specifications. But love's expression fulfills God's requirement because we continue to express our devotion as long as we have love.

The person who has never read the Bible can fulfill the moral law in its general meaning. Nothing is required of us in our man-to-man relationship that is not motivated by love. Paul is emphatic on this: "Owe no man anything, save to love one another: for he that loveth his neighbor hath fulfilled the law. For this, Thou shalt not commit adultery, Thou shalt not kill, Thou shalt not steal, Thou shalt not covet, and if there be any other commandment, it is summed up in this word, namely, Thou shalt love thy neighbor as thyself. Love worketh no ill to his neighbor: love therefore is the fulfillment of the law" (Romans 13:8-10).

If a person loves his neighbor he will not steal his money or his wife; he will not kill him or lie to him. This is the negative expression. In a positive expression Jesus said, "All things therefore whatsoever ye would that men do unto you, even so do ye also unto them: for this is the law and the prophets" (Matt. 7:12).

"This is the law and the prophets." "On these two commandments the whole law hangeth, and the prophets." Through the centuries, God has been trying to get us to love Him and one another. That was the intent of the Law of Moses and the message of the prophets. Love fulfills the purpose of God's laws.

3. A legal code specifies, defines, and enumerates. When one meets the specifications, he is legally righteous and free from further demands of the law. How often must I assemble and how much time must I spend there? How often and how long must I pray? How much must I give? What is the minimum in meeting the law's demands? Love is not concerned with minimums. What is the minimum that a righteous man may do for his wife and children? He is not concerned about minimums. What is the maximum that God accepts? I can give you a more definite answer to this question. God will accept all you are and all you have. He accepted the last two coins of a widow. They were not required legally, but they were accepted as a love offering. God accepted the life of Stephen.

One man will sell his possessions, uproot his family, wear himself out raising support, take his children from their grandparents, and go into a land of poverty and filth among people of strange language and customs and expend himself and his family in an effort to save the lost. Another man will not become involved in his own congregation. What makes the difference in these two men? Does law demand more of one than the other? No, but love motivates one more than the other.

Suppose that I am driving down a highway that crosses a body of water. I see a car plunge off the bridge into the water. There are six persons in it who cannot swim. I stop and hurriedly jump in and pull one person out. Then I go in and rescue another. I am doing a marvelous thing. A third person is pulled out. I am becoming a hero. They will have me on the six o'clock news on Channel 4. Again I plunge in and rescue a fourth person. Then I say to myself, "I think I have done my part now. I have saved more people than most people do in a lifetime. Now I think it is time for somebody else to do his part." Then I let the other two drown. Now, am I a hero?—or a criminal? Love does not ask, "What is required?" It asks, "How can I serve?" The same concern will be shown for all as long as there is love, need, and ability.

Love seeks the good of others instead of seeking to comply with regulations. This is righteousness in the heart rather than legal justification.

4. I was brought up on the "Christian duty" concept. All facets of discipleship became one's duty. And when a person forsook the Lord, he was "out of duty". Such a concept is foreign to the New Testament. The "do your duty" approach is an effort to pay an obligation to God by meeting His legal demands. A hired hand performs duties. The employer specifies, "You do these four things and then I will pay you so much." When the employee does the four specified things, he has fulfilled his duty and earned his pay. Nothing more can be demanded of his time or effort. He is free from the employer. And he can do all this with no love for the employer. So it is with us when we try to fulfill our discipleship through specified tithes, hours, and quotas instead of a full expression of love.

Jesus spoke of duty only once. He said in Luke 17:10, "Even so ye also, when ye shall have done all the things that are commanded you, say, We are unprofitable servants; we have done that which it was our duty to do." A person might become convinced that a tithe, or higher percentage, is required. He could pay that out of a sense of lawful duty with little or no love. But then whose would the remainder of his income be? Would he be free from the constraining influence of love in the use of it?

While improperly motivated people may speak of duty, responsibility, and obligation, love speaks of opportunity. Love seeks opportunity to express itself. "So then, as we have opportunity, let us work that which is good toward all men, and especially toward them that are of the household of faith" (Gal. 6:10). Thus, love transcends any sense of duty.

After amplifying these four reasons why love is the great commandment, it is easy to understand why Jesus would choose love to be the identifying characteristic of His disciples. (This, my favorite and most used lesson, was inspired by Edward J. Craddock in 1945 in Beaumont, Texas.)

Chapter 5

SOMETHING GREATER THAN LAW

Even the most rigid of God's laws were not always inflexible. There are examples showing that in certain circumstances there was elasticity in the most absolute laws. In this lesson we shall look for the principles which take precedence over law.

These references call for respect for Old Testament laws. "You shall not add to the word which I command you, nor take from it," God warned Israel (Deut. 4:1f). The writer of Hebrews reminds us that "every transgression or disobedience received a just retribution" (Heb. 2:1f). "A man who has violated the law of Moses dies without mercy . . . " (Heb. 10:28). Jesus adds His warning about tampering with the law, "Whoever then relaxes one of the least of these commandments and teaches men so, shall be called least in the kingdom of heaven" (Matt. 5:19).

Similar warning is given concerning observance of Jesus' teachings. "He who rejects me and does not receive my sayings has a judge: the word that I have spoken will be his judge on the last day" (John 12:48). While making disciples, the apostles were to be "teaching them to observe all that I have commanded you" (Matt. 28:19). James adds rigidity to those words, saying, "Whoever keeps the whole law but fails in one point has become guilty of all of it" (James 2:10).

These passages seem plain enough. We must respect God's laws. But there are also examples of flexibility of God's laws. These have been overlooked usually. Let us investigate some of them.

"You shall not bear false witness against your neighbor" (Exo. 20:16) is God's law against dishonesty. The rigidity of that law is reinforced by God's treatment of Ananias and Sapphira who lied (Acts 5:1-11). But the Bible gives record of other persons who were dishonest and were not punished. I choose this one example because it is approved. Rahab lied and deceived in protecting the spies (Josh. 2:1f). Yet she is listed among the heroes of faith for that very reason: "By faith Rahab the harlot did not perish with those who were disobedient, because she had given friendly welcome to the spies" (Heb. 11:31).

The articles of furniture in the tabernacle were holy, and they were to be touched by no one (Num. 4:15f). The twelve loaves of bread placed on the table of showbread were holy also and were to be eaten only by Aaron and his sons. Uzzah was killed instantly by the Lord when he touched the Ark of the Covenant (2 Sam. 6:6f). But David and his soldiers ate the bread of the Presence and Jesus gave His approval of the action (Matt. 12:1f; Mk.2:23f; Lk. 6:1f).

God made the sabbath a day of rest, free from all labor (Exo. 20:8f). Later, a man was arrested for gathering sticks on the sabbath. His offense was made a test case for the absolute quality of the sabbath law. At God's direction, he was stoned to death for his violation (Num. 15:32f).

A Test Case

The Jews accepted the sabbath law as rigid and arbitrary. Out of respect for it, they made the most technical definitions of what could or could not be done on the sabbath. In the time of Moses the test case had been made of the sabbath law which the Jews interpreted as proving its rigidity. However, Jesus chose the sabbath law as a test case to show its flexibility and elasticity, giving way to the weightier matters of the law. Six times Jesus did things on the sabbath which were called in question by his legalistic critics. Jesus was deliberate in this, making an emphatic point. He was showing the true nature of law. Jesus was denying the arbitrary nature of law, declaring that there is something greater than law. Jesus was saying that God thinks more highly of mercy extended to a cow or donkey than to the sabbath law (Luke 13:10f; 18:1f). It is hard for a Pharisee to grasp that!

If you are bedfast, must you assemble with the saints? Where do the Scriptures excuse one because of "providential hindrance," as though God would hinder anyone? Jesus rebuked the legalists of His day for tithing with absolute strictness while leaving undone the "weightier matters of the law" of justice, mercy, faith, and love (Matt. 23:23f; Luke 11:42). The demands of law are met by demonstration of love (Rom. 13:8f). If we understand a law to conflict with mercy and love, we have misintrepeted the law. These fundamental principles should prevail for they are the purpose of the law. Jesus made a deliberate issue of this, using the sabbath law as the test case. The most rigid of laws was chosen to set forth the principle.

In the three illustrations used earlier, this principle prevailed. Rahab was promoting the causes of justice and faith by her deceit. David and his famished men, fighting for a just cause, could not have been denied the only available food with mercy. Jesus' actions on the sabbath were all unselfish expressions of mercy, which mercy could be shown to an unfortunate, suffering animal on the sabbath.

It would be too tedious and it would require too much space to include the Biblical narrative of each of the six sabbath confrontations. We will list them here for your more thorough investigation.

1. In the grainfield (Matt. 12:1f; Mk. 2:23f; Lk. 6:1f). "I desire mercy, and not sacrifice." "The Son of man is lord of the sabbath." "The sabbath was made for man, and not man for the sabbath."

2. Healing the man with the withered hand (Matt. 12:9f; Mk. 3:1f; Lk. 6:6f). "It is lawful to do good on the sabbath."

3. Healing at Bethesda (John 5:1f).

4. Healing of the blind man at Siloam (John 9:1f).

5. Healing a woman with an infirmity (Lk. 13:10f). "Does not each of you on the sabbath untie his ox or his ass from the manger, and lead it away to water?"

6. Healing the man with dropsy (Lk. 14:1f). "Which of you, having an ass or an ox that has fallen into a well, will not immediately pull him out on a sabbath day?"

Jesus was showing that the Jews proclaimed rigidity but accepted some elasticity in law, just as we do. Jesus justified his actions by these accepted examples:

1. David ate showbread which was unlawful for him to eat. (Matt. 12:4).

2. Priests work in the temple on the sabbath (Matt. 12:5).

3. Priests circumcise on the sabbath (John 7:22f).

4. A sheep would be lifted out of a pit on the sabbath (Matt. 12:10).

5. Animals are untied and led to water on the sabbath (Luke 14:5).

6. An ox or a donkey would be pulled out of a well on the sabbath (Lk. 13:15).

Was Jesus justifying "doing evil that good may come" (Rom. 3:8)? These actions were not evil. These "violations" became good because of the higher motives which prompted them. The purpose of the law — the weightier matters of the law — was served. The laws of God are against neither animals nor men. Jesus went to great length to put this message across, but we are slow to grasp it because we have been conditioned to the keeping of arbitrary details for our justification.

Jesus explained, "The sabbath was made for man, and not man for the sabbath." The law was made for the good of man. Man was not made to fit arbitrary laws. If, in a specific instance, our efforts to keep a law hinders or prevents the principles of justice, mercy, faith, or love, then the higher principle must take precedence. The principle is greater than the law intended to promote it.

When we come to making application of this to specific situations, we find that there are many hard decisions. Sometimes it is easier to keep legal specifics than to make responsible decisions. In making decisions, we must be sure that we are making the most unselfish and loving choice serving the best interest of the most persons involved.

To demand that a person assemble when ill or leave a dying loved one to attend services would be unmerciful. It would likewise be unmerciful to demand that a person with laryngitis sing, or to deprive aged parents or destitute neighbors in order to be able to "lay by in store."

It would be unjust, unmerciful, and unloving to refuse to save your family from a deranged or criminal attacker either by deceit or use of force which might take the life of the attacker. You may protest that no one has the right to kill, but that the attacker should only be scared away or injured. But where do you get permission to deceive the attacker by scaring him with an unloaded gun or to injure him?

It would also be unjust, unmerciful, and unloving to fail to defend loved ones, home, and country from invaders. This kind of defense might take many forms.

"Pulling the plug" has become a topic of many discussions and some court decisions. Some of us have been called upon to make decision as to the extent of heroic effort to be made to keep a terminal case alive. We are not "playing God" when we make responsible decisions for God has put life and death in our hands. To bring life into the world irresponsibly is as immoral as to end life irresponsibly. When the cause of love, justice, and mercy has been served, God has always respected man's decisions and actions, even to the taking of life.

Our fox terrier was a part of our family for thirteen years. You know the feeling for such a pet. He became hopelessly diseased with lukemia. My family made the decision. We gave Ol' Cisco a tearful farewell and let the veterinarian put him to sleep. If we can show such compassion to an animal, can we not let one whom we love dearly die with dignity and mercy?

Perhaps we should reappraise the matter of suicide in this context. Suicide is not dealt with in the Scriptures, so it must be judged by principles. Some have taken their own lives out of psychotic compulsion. God will judge them mercifully because of that mental disorder.

Although they did not perform the acts of violence which took their lives, many have given their lives as a loving act, choosing death for the highest reasons. Jesus said, "Greater love has no man than this, that a man lay down his life for his friends" (John 15:13). Of His own choosing to die, He said, "For this reason the Father loves me, because I lay down my life, that I may take it again. No one takes it from me, but I lay it down of my own accord" (John 10:17f). He consented to die and accepted the responsibility for it in a totally loving and unselfish choice.

There is an example of one person performing the violent act which took his life, and his name is recorded in Inspirations's Hall of Fame because of it. It was an unselfish act promoting the cause of justice for God's people. That man's name was Samson (Heb. 11:32f).

At this point you may be wishing to remind me of 1 Corinthians 3:16-17: "Do you not know that you are God's temple and that God's Spirit dwells in you? If any one destroys God's temple, God will destroy him. For God's temple is holy, and that you are." This has been our proof-text against destroying our bodies by smoking, drinking, and other vices. But that is a misapplication, for the whole context reveals that it refers to the church rather than the human body. At Corinth they were destroying Christ's body by sectarian divisions. First Corinthians 6:19-20 does refer to the human body as a temple, but it does not speak of its being destroyed. It concludes, "So glorify God in your body." That's what Samson did in his self-destruction.

Abortion is a big issue now. It is not mentioned in the Bible. No one can prove when life begins by the Bible. And that is not necessary, except for the legalist. In each circumstance, decision can best be made by asking, "What is the most loving, just, and merciful choice for those involved?" It is not an easy decision, but it will be a responsible one.

Jesus did not give us who try to be marriage counsellors all of the easy solutions for the marriage-divorce-remarriage problems. In many cases the involvements are so complex that we can only ask what decision serves the purpose of the law best.

Can we go too far astray when we in all circumstances make decisions based on the "weightier matters of the law"? Some may decry this as situation ethics or brand it with some other prejudicial disparagement, but Jesus deliberately took the sabbath law as a test case to teach this lesson. Our preoccupation with legal justification has blinded our eyes to this great truth. Yes, there is something greater than law.

In Christ we are free to make responsible decisions in the world of men with the assurance that God recognizes our unselfish and loving motives and smiles His approval.

Chapter 6

LAWYERS

Someone has observed that God has not called us to be lawyers, but lovers.

We in the Church of Christ have developed some strange concepts of Christ's law. We seem to conceive of a system of law half revealed and half concealed in biography, historical accounts, treatises, personal letters, and prophecy. Clues to the laws are scattered through these writings to be discovered, pieced together, and interpreted by studious lawyers of the Word. We must not trust anyone else for this, we are cautioned, though his talents, training, and dedication may be much greater than ours. We must become lawyers ourselves. Lack of literacy or academic training is no excuse.

It is like a child's puzzle — a maze. If you are astute enough, you can be among the spiritually elite who are able to work their way through the maze. But if you make a wrong turn, which most religious people presumably have done, then you will find yourself in the dead end of eternal punishment. That is the verdict, at least, the lawyers of the Word render as they put on their robes and sit in judgment of all others. The majority of the most learned, sincere, and devoted students of the Word are lost in the interpretative maze, while lots of us simple folk breeze right on through to eternal glory.

Such an approach to interpretation as I have described has been drilled into us for most of this century. How appalling! How sad!

Most of the disciples of Jesus through the centuries did not even have a Bible to study, and they could not have read it if they had owned one. They could not have become lawyers. They had to depend upon the public reading and explanations. Surely, they did not understand it all, and they did not all understand it alike. But this was not necessary unless their justification was dependent upon keeping the details of a legal code. This is where we have made the wrong turn in our maze and have dead-ended short of the goal.

Legalistic interpretation has made our stress on Bible study a farce. The Sunday morning auditorium class is filled with persons who have been "studying" for years and years. Yet they give the most simplistic, and often incorrect, answers, and they still disagree on many of the issues listed in Chapter One.

In this lesson we shall consider three ways that we have gone astray in our approach to interpretation of the message.

The Legal Approach

Let me illustrate our legal approach to interpretation by this description of a disciple of Christ:

A disciple of Christ must be a man of faith and conviction. He must love his wife and children and rear his children in the faith. He must provide for his family. He must pay his debts. He must deal fairly with his employees. He must love his enemies. He must read and study his Bible. He must assemble regularly and lay by in store each week. His speech must be becoming a disciple, etc.

Other than this being an incomplete description of a disciple of Christ, you probably pick no flaw with anything in the paragraph. You understand that I am giving a general description.

But how wrong can you be! There are one or more flaws in each sentence! A disciple of Christ does not have to be a man; it can be a girl. A wife and children are not necessary; an unmarried person can be a disciple. He does not need a family to provide for to qualify. Neither must he or she have debts, nor pay debts if that person is destitute or disabled. Enemies are unnecessary to qualify. He or she need not be literate or scholarly, or attend services if bedfast, etc. Yet, each of those qualities was listed as a "must."

Each sentence contains one or more flaws if you consider the paragraph to be giving lawful specifications. But you understood it properly when you interpreted it as a general description of a disciple. What a difference a legalistic approach to interpretation makes! Legalism misses the general concept and emphasizes the details as arbitrary, escalating them to life-and-death issues. It results in endless controversy and hair-splitting. It is a built-in system for dividing people.

Now, with this in mind, please read Paul's description of an elder in 1 Timothy 3:1-7 and Titus 1:5-9. Do you not see the description in a different light? Now you can see that Paul was only directing the selection of men of spiritual maturity, reputation, and ability to teach and minister to the welfare of the congregation. He is not giving a checklist of legal details.

When a move is made within a congregation to appoint elders, what is the first thing we all look for? We look for men who have two baptized children. In more daring congregations they settle for one child instead of two. Now, think of this: we are in need of men of spiritual maturity, good reputation, and ability to teach and lead, and we ask who has a baptized child or two. That's really good thinking, isn't it! In numerous cases we have passed over the most qualified men in the church because they were not blessed with a child. The Lord only knows how the church has suffered because of our legalistic hangup.

Timothy was at Ephesus when Paul wrote describing the kind of men who should be appointed as bishops. If Timothy went ahead and appointed men according to Paul's qualifications, did he necessarily appoint men with believing children. Certainly not! He had no such instructions from Paul. Paul had written, "He must manage his own household well, keeping his children submissive and respectful in every way; for if a man does not know how to manage his own household, how can he care for God's church?" (1 Tim. 3:4). Nothing is said about believing children.

You may wish to remind me that Paul stipulated to Titus that "his children are believers" (Titus 1:6). That is true, but Timothy did not have that letter. Evidently, the letters to Timothy and Titus were written about the same time. Timothy was at Ephesus and Titus was on the island of Crete. Timothy would have no reason to, and could not, call Titus on the phone to compare the descriptions. He could not compile the two descriptions. He had no need to. He was no legalist.

The two descriptions are not synoptic like the biographies of Jesus; neither were the lists lawful specifications, else both lists would necessarily be identical. Try matching the details in two columns side by side and see how diverse they are. Yet Timothy and Titus could recognize the general kind of person that Paul was characterizing.

Surely, if a man had children who were disobedient or rebellious, that would disqualify him. Because he had two obedient teenagers, however, who lived under his parental training and authority since their first breaths, that would not mean that he knew how to oversee a congregation of many adults. We could make a better case for his need of being successful in business. A man's household evidently included his servants. That was his business operation. Managing his business/household well would show his ability to deal with people effectively.

"It is too risky to appoint a man who has no children," someone warns. Do you think Timothy would have considered it a risk to use Paul's instructions to him? It is risky to pass over the person who can lead the congregation effectively in favor of an inept leader who has two children. The church has suffered enough from such unbalanced priorities based on legal interpretation.

Inconsistency

Another interpretative weakness is our lack of consistency in applying the same rules and principles to similar cases. I remember the "bobbed hair" controversy when I was a teenager. Women had begun to cut their hair and they were brazen enough to worship God unveiled — that is, without a hat on. Outside of our fellowship, women would lead in services publicly and teach and preach. In the Church of Christ women began to teach in classes.

Many discussions were had by devout people who wanted to be right with God above all else. In time, we came to accept an interpretation of First Corinthians 11 on the basis of custom. Considering the custom in Corinth with its prostitute priestesses serving the great pagan temple, we could understand why Paul would forbid their removing their veil and cutting their hair like the priestesses. Now circumstance and custom have changed and there is no significance attached to headdress or hairstyle. We understand that customs of dress are not binding for all ages and localities. That is a sensible interpretation. It does not bind arbitrary details.

When we come to First Corinthians 14, however, we quickly abandon that approach to interpretation. The silence of women becomes an unchanging, universal, arbitrary specific of law. The city, people, circumstance, and custom are the same. The only difference is that one relates to headdress and the other relates to teaching publicly. Paul appeals to the loftiest of principles, the headship of man and the submission of woman, on which to base his binding the veil and the prohibiting of teaching. Can we say that we have been consistent in applying the same rule in like circumstances?

Our instruction to greet one another with a holy kiss is rather plain, being repeated five times (Rom. 16:16; 1 Cor. 16:20; 2 Cor. 13:12; 1 Thes. 5:26; 1 Pet. 5:14). We feel at ease in substituting a method which conveys the meaning of what we are instructed to do. So we shake hands instead of kissing. Can we do this consistently while refusing to allow an alteration of the method by which the meaning of baptism is expressed?

Our burial with Christ is figurative. "We are buried with him" (Rom. 6:4; Col. 2:12). It is likely that you visualize that Jesus is symbolically buried in the baptistry with the candidate, but Jesus is not buried with us; it is we with Him. Jesus was buried, not in water, but in a rock-hewn tomb. In baptism, symbolically, one is transported back through time and space and buried with Christ where atonement was made. So the burial is in the tomb. The action of baptism symbolizes that. To millions of persons, dipping, pouring, or sprinkling of water ritually symbolizes that action.

These points about baptism are made, not to convince you of the validity of dipping the head, pouring, or sprinkling for baptism, but to make you less dogmatic against one who is convinced that these forms are acceptable expressions. It makes us uncomfortable to face our inconsistency.

Scholasticism

Through the early centuries, the Catholic church, claiming church authority, added many practices without Scriptural foundation. The reformers later pressed for Scriptural authority for all practices. So a form of defense called scholasticism was employed. This scholasticism was an effort to prove by the Bible what had already been accepted and practiced traditionally.

This device is widely used, allowing one to "search the Scriptures," grasping passages, and making them accommodate the need. Proof-texts are taken from their context and made to support something that the writer did not have in mind. Texts are made to prove too much.

We in the Church of Christ have denounced others for this practice while blind to the fact that we were among the chief offenders. I shall use only one illustration of this interpretative flaw used by the lawyers of the Word.

From the secular writers of the early centuries, it seems evident that very early disciples began to use the first day of the week as a special day for assembly and devotion. This was such an accepted practice that, at the end of the persecutions in the fourth century, Constantine declared Sunday to be a holiday (holy day) for the benefit of Christians. From that time the first day of the week had been a holiday for worship in Christian countries. We accepted it also, defining it to the point of declaring it to be the only day on which one could give money or commune acceptably. Sunday assemblies became more necessary than those on weekdays. Many made a kind of sabbath out of it, forbidding any work or recreation on Sunday. It has become such an accepted special day that few among us would dare question that it is clearly defined and stipulated in the Scriptures.

When it is questioned, what evidences are offered for its support? Jesus arose on the first day and the church began on the first day. That is interesting, but it is not proof, and no inspired writer gave that as a reason why we must emphasize the first day. Well, the disciples came together to break bread at Troas on the first day (Acts 20:7). We dealt with this point in Chapter Two. It does not indicate that they were commanded to do that, that they had been doing it previously, or that they continued to meet on the first day thereafter. The only thing Acts 20:7 proves on the subject is that it is permissible to meet on Sunday.

-40-

Then there is 1 Corinthians 16:2: "Upon the first day of every week, each of you is to put something aside and store it up, as he may prosper, so that contributions need not be made when I come." That says nothing about an assembly; it calls for individual action. While it may seem reasonable that Paul chose the first day of the week for storing because they assembled then, that is not the stated case. It is equally reasonable to conclude that this time was chosen because a person received his wages at the end of the week and would be urged to a systematic storing up at home at that time.

These two passages are the only mention made of the first day in connection with activity of the disciples

There is nothing to identify "the day" (Heb. 10:25) and "the Lord's day" (Rev. 1:10) as the first day of the week. Really, if the Lord had intended that the first day of the week be a special day for worship, don't you think He would have told us? He would not have obscured such a vital demand in vague inference for lawyers to find.

Our people have berated others for observing special days like Christmas and Easter, being naively unaware that we are the ones who "esteem one day as better than another" (Rom. 14:5). Approach to God in worship and service is limited "neither on this mountain nor in Jerusalem" (John 4:21) nor on certain days.

Admittedly, the recognition of this traditional day of worship by governments of Western nations has been a great blessing to those serving Christ.

Why do we make such a defense for the first day of the week? It is a part of our tendency to define lawful requirements so we can fulfill them. It is a part of legalism. When we determine the purposes to be accomplished by assemblies, we also can see that these purposes can be fulfilled on any day of the week. We do not meet because it is the first day and we are required to do so; we meet to fulfill the purposes to be accomplished in assemblies.

As lawyers of the Word, we have interpreted the Scriptures as a legal system; we have been inconsistent in our application of principles of interpretation, and we have supported our traditional practices by scholasticism. These practices are much more inclusive than the few examples in this lesson.

There is much more flexibility and adaptability, and much less pattern, than we who are conditioned by legalism can recognize or accept with ease. But this awareness and acceptance is a part of the happiness that comes by being free in Christ.

When we look upon the Scriptures as a code of laws and begin to try to interpret them as such, we become lawyers. Then we become judges of those who do not accept our interpretations. In so doing, we miss the spirit of the message.

Chapter 7

THE EXERCISE OF CHRISTIAN LIBERTY

"For freedom did Christ set us free: stand fast therefore, and be not entangled again in a yoke of bondage" (Gal. 5:1). In Christ men have liberty befitting sons of God. Such was not true of those bound by the Mosaic "handle not, nor touch, nor taste." Under the Law, a person could be defiled by non-moral things. Guilt was incurred by the touching of a dead animal or a piece of holy furniture or by the tasting of pork.

I. Can Non-moral Things and Actions be Sinful?

Our purity or defilement is not determined by what we see, hear, taste, or touch, but by our motive for seeing, hearing tasting, and touching. Jesus explained that man is defiled by his thoughts rather than by what he eats (Matt. 15:1:20). Defilement is not in certain actions and things, but in improper use of and attitude toward those actions and things. Actions and things, generally speaking, are non-moral. They have no inherent moral value. Is not this the point that Paul would impress upon us? "I know, and am persuaded in the Lord Jesus, that nothing is unclean of itself: save that to him who accounteth anything to be unclean, to him it is unclean . . . for the kingdom of God is not eating and drinking, but righteousness and peace and joy in the Holy Spirit" (Rom. 14:14-17). Our purity of thought or defilement of purpose determines whether a thing is moral or immoral. Sin is not in things, but in people — in the heart. This is what Paul expressed when he wrote, "To the pure all things are pure: but to them that are defiled and unbelieving nothing is pure; but both their mind and their conscience are defiled" (Titus 1:15). Shakespeare only expressesd this truth when he said, "Nothing is good or bad, but thinking makes it so."

To show the non-moral nature of actions and things, some examples are listed. These all show that the thought, or motive, determines whether it is right or wrong.

1. The taking of life is judged by the purity or defilement of heart. The person who kills accidentally or defensively, having no impure heart in it, remains pure in the act. It is not so with the man who kills with hatred or anger although he performs the identical act of the first man.

2. One person may use narcotics for medical purposes and be justified while the person with defiled purpose takes them for their thrilling effects.

3. Alcoholic beverage, when taken for curative purposes or in moderation, does not defile as it does when taken for intoxication. The act is the same; the difference is in the heart.

4. A person, desiring to know more about religious doctrines, may in purity go to a service where error is being taught or may subscribe to such a periodical or buy such a book. He is not judged like the person who gives mental consent to the destrctive error while performing the same acts.

5. Two men may look upon a woman with strong desire toward her, one being pure, the other guilty of sin. One desires to have her as his wife; the other desires to satisfy his lusts.

6. Two persons may take part in a competitive game or attend a sporting activity with different prospects. One purposes to enjoy the activity while the other wishes to gamble.

7. One preacher may preach to save souls while the other tries to build himself up in honor by preaching. Though the sermons may be identical, the motive made one right and the other wrong.

All of these examples show that the act itself is non-moral. Its merit or demerit is determined by the heart. "To the pure all things are pure, but to them that are defiled and unbelieving, nothing is pure."

II. Principles Governing Liberty in Non-moral Things

When a new kind of case is tried in the courts, it becomes a "test case". The decision rendered toward it is used to judge all other cases which involve a like principle. There are two test cases in the Scriptures regarding Christian liberty. These both involve non-moral things — the eating of food and circumcision. The verdict in regard to the eating of meats demands (1) that a Christian surrender his liberties if they put a fellow disciple in jeopardy, and (2) that his liberty be exercised with self-control. In regards to circumcision, the verdict forbids us to bind our scruples on others so as to limit their Christian liberty. These verdicts can be applied to everything which is of like principle today. (Read 1 Cor. 6, 8, 10; Rom. 14; all of Galatians; Acts 15).

III. Our Liberty is Limited by Self-Control

Man must never be brought under the control of anything of a non-moral nature. "All things are lawful for me; but I will not be brought under the power of any. Meats for the belly, and the belly for meats; but God shall bring to nought both it and them" (1 Cor. 6:12-13). Paul is saying, "God has created the body with its appetites, cravings, and desires, and at the same time God created good things to satisfy the desires; let the desires be fulfilled in moderation and self-control, not slavishly being ruled by the desires." Both the appetite and the meat to satisfy are non-moral. They have no special significance before God. "But food will not commend us to God: neither, if we eat not, are we the worse; nor, if we eat, are we the better" (1 Cor. 8:8). Applying this principle to all instincts, desires, drives, or cravings given by God, we see that none are evil within themselves. Consider these.

1. The instinct of self-preservation. It is right to preserve ourselves, to seek for our own well-being, unless we let the desire control us causing us to become fraudulent, deceptive, greedy, injurious to others, or disrespectful of the rights of others.

2. Desire for food. This is a pure thing unless we lose control of the desire and become gluttonous or steal for food to eat. Because it is abused by some does not make it sinful to desire, obtain, and eat food.

3. Desire of approval. It is natural and right for us to want others to think well of us. This makes us good neighbors. If this desire controls us, we may become hypocritical, deceitful, or extravagant in order to gain approval.

4. Desire to possess. This is the instinct God gave us to cause us to provide for our needs. If one is "brought under the power

of" the desire, he may become a thief, coveteous, stingy, or an extortioner, or he may destroy his health in order to possess. The flagrant abuse by some does not make the proper exercise of the instinct unholy in others. The pure heart will permit only the proper exercise of the drive.

5. Mating instinct. The desire for sexual fulfillment is given by God for the establishment of the home and the propagation of the race through marriage. If, through lack of self-control, one is brought under the power of his instinct so as to become lustful or immoral, he has abused God's arrangement.

6. Reaching out for God. It is a natural desire in man to worship a higher power. Misdirected and out of control, this natural drive has led most of mankind away from the true God. The desire in man is not condemned because it is abused by the majority.

In all these things man has free exercise of liberty so long as his heart is kept pure and self-control is maintained. For this cause Paul emphasized the necessity of the mind's mastery over the flesh. This brings the war in our members: "But I say, Walk by the Spirit, and ye shall not fulfil the lust of the flesh. For the flesh lusteth against the Spirit, and the Spirit against the flesh; for these are contrary the one to the other; that ye may not do the things that ye would" (Gal. 5:16-17). So he says, "For ye, brethren, were called for freedom, only use not your freedom for an occasion to the flesh" (Gal. 5:13).

Is everything that could lead to sin evil? The affirmative answer to this has led many people to censor many non-moral activities while inconsistently sanctioning other practices of the same nature. Any non-moral activity could lead to sin.

1. The preparation and enjoyment of wholesome meals could, and often does, lead to over-eating. Must one refuse to eat? To prepare a fine meal for guests may lead them to over-eat. Should one ration the meal of his company?

2. Working at a job and earning a good salary might lead a person to love money.

3. Even though some have had wine prescribed for them by a doctor, they refused it on the ground that it could lead to sin.

The contention is true, but does that justify the restraint of the liberty?

4. All kinds of competitive games are used as an instrument for gambling. Any game could lead to gambling. Who can say which game would tempt a person to gamble more than others? Must one refrain from all games and sporting events?

5. Many have fallen into immorality and adultery while selecting a companion. Courting can, and often does, lead to sin. Should the young person let his parents choose his companion for him so as to avoid this possibility?

6. Over three hundred million people declare that the study of the Bible leads to sin by misunderstanding it through private interpretion. The claim is true. More people who read it misunderstand it than understand it. But does that censor the act of reading the Bible?

We cannot destroy the desires, drives, and instincts discussed earlier. In exercising them, we should "watch and pray that you enter not into temptation." We must strengthen ourselves to live as Christians worthy of the honor Christ bestowed on us as free sons, not as servants under a yoke of bondage. Here we see the necessity of purity of mind and purpose, of mental discipline and self-control. "For God gave us not a spirit of fearfulness; but of power and love and discipline" (2 Tim. 1:7). Disciples must be taught to respect the high calling and liberty that God has extended to them. Purity of heart will maintain an enlivened conscience toward all things. Pinocchio let Jiminy Cricket be his conscience. A disciple should not let the preacher, or anyone else, be his conscience. He must have one of his own. Until this is developed in a congregation, it is futile to try to herd it by the preacher's conscience.

IV. Liberty is Limited by a Charitable Regard For Others

Love would constrain a disciple to surrender his liberty in non-moral things if they prove to be destructive to a brother. "All things are lawful for me; but not all things are expedient" (1 Cor. 6:12; 10:23). "Overthrow not for meats sake the work of God. All things indeed are clean; howbeit it is evil for that man who eateth with offence. It is good not to eat flesh, nor to drink wine, nor to do anything whereby thy brother stumbleth" (Rom. 14:20-21). Urging that we be above blame in exercising our liberties, Paul exhorts, "Let not your good be evil spoken of" (Rom. 14:16). "Happy is he that condemneth not himself in that which he alloweth: (Rom. 14:22). Freedom must not destroy others.

The test case to illustrate this is the eating of meats which had been sacrificed to idols. Realizing that meat cannot contaminate him spiritually, the disciple could eat such meat with no regard to the idol. But a weak brother who has just escaped from idolatry, seeing his brother eat the meat, thinks that he is eating with regard to the idol. Being thus misinformed, he may be led to eat with respect to the idol. Thus he has been encouraged to sin by his unsuspecting brother. If the man is aware of the weak brother's conviction, he should not eat. This does not forever ban the man from eating meat, however. After he instructs the weak brother properly, the temptation will have been taken away and he can continue to exercise that liberty.

"Wherefore, if meat causeth my brother to stumble, I will eat no flesh for evermore, that I cause not my brother to stumble" (1 Cor. 8:13). Did Paul become a vegetarian? Or did he not use discretion in his eating and continue to teach the truth about Christian liberty? Continuing his discussion into Chapter 9, he declared his right to eat and drink.

Out of regard for our brother, practices which put undue strain on his weakness must be avoided. Even our laws hold us liable for creating attractive hazards such as leaving a ladder up where a child might climb and fall. Although teasing a person is a non-moral thing, it would be wrong to tease a temperamental person until he becomes angry and loses his temper. This class of activity is practiced without evil motive, but it shows lack of regard for others and is not expedient because it may cause the death of a brother.

V. Liberty of Others Must Be Respected

We have not the right to limit the liberty of others by binding our scruples on them. The Jewish disciples had a doctrinal conviction that the custom of circumcision should be bound

(Acts 15:1). Others realized that "in Christ Jesus neither cir-cumcision availeth anything, nor uncircumcision" (Gal. 5:6). Circumcision, in itself, is a non-moral thing, neither helping nor hindering. But the binding of this scruple was about to split the whole church. These Judaizers "came in privily to spy out our liberty which we have in Christ Jesus, that they might bring us into bondage . . . " (Gal. 2:4). Did Paul say, "Oh, well, since circumcision really does not make any difference, we had better surrender our liberty and accept this yoke lest the church be split through the offense of these brethren"? He did not! " . . . To whom we gave place in the way of subjection, no, not for an hour" (Gal. 2:5).

Almost alone the great Paul waged this battle for our freedom in Christ. Even Peter had about surrendered (Gal. 2:11-13). Because he so detested this yoke of bondage, Paul's apostleship was being questioned by some. This Judaism had invaded Anti-och. From there it would envelop all of Paul's work among the Gentiles. What should he do? A battle had to be fought to keep us free. God sent him to the fight (Gal. 2:2; Acts 15). He won a victory for us today.

If they could bind circumcision, others can bring us into bon-dage to their scruples in demanding that our liberties be limited in studying in classes, using individual cups for communion, helping the fatherless, cooperating in evangelization, building up a large congregation, having food in fellowship in the build-ing, and what else might be your local problem. Although the abuse of any non-moral exercise — and these are all non-moral — can lead to sin, we are not condemned by a sensible exercise of it.

Now that the battle is won, what attitude will Paul de-monstrate? Rather than further driving the wedge to split the church, he made concessions to them to promote healing by love. After proving that circumcision could not be bound on Titus, he took Timothy "and circumcised him because of the Jews" (Acts 16:3).

Then later, Paul took up a collection from these Gentiles and took it back to the very ones who were excluding them from the kindom of God. He must have had more motive in this than charity toward the poor. On bearing this gift to Jerusalem, he agreed to purify himself in the temple as a concession to make peace (Acts 21:26). All of this was done after he had won his case. Charitable concessions can be made without the surrender of liberty. These are necessary to preserve the unity of believers.

Principles cannot be applied with legalism. They are applied through personal judgment. "Circumstances alter cases." So Paul exhorts, " . . . be perfected together in the same mind and in the same judgment. (1 Cor. 1:10). And, "The faith which thou hast, have to thyself before God" (Rom. 14:22). Also, "But him that is weak in faith, receive ye, yet not for decision of scruples" (Rom. 14:1).

If we were to be bound by the scruples of everyone, we could not drink tea, coffee, or Coke, chew gum, read the funny paper, tell a joke, see any sort of entertainment, read a magazine, play any games, spend any money on pleasure, and so on without end. But few of these restrictions would be due to the scruples of the weak brother. They would come from preachers, elders, and other staunch individuals who would limit our liberty by binding their convictions on us.

VI. Evil Displayed with the Good

Must a thing be shunned because evil is displayed with the good? Again, purity of purpose determines the case. Only the good will be sought by the pure in heart. But evil is everywhere. In one form or another it is presented in the newspaper, on the radio, on television, in movies, in fiction, in history, in the Bible, in the school, in places of business, on the job, at the game, in the church, and in the home.

In all of these things our purpose is to accept the good while holding misgivings toward the evils incidental to the good. The desirable rose has thorns incidental to it. Although the thorns are detested, we do not let them prohibit enjoyment of the rose. In enjoying the rose, we learn to avoid the prick of the thorn. So the presence of that which is undesirable does not eliminate our liberty to enjoy that which is good.

VII. CONCLUSION

"For freedom did Christ set us free: stand fast therefore, and be not entangled again in a yoke of bondage." In exercising our

liberty in Christ, we must not come into bondage to:
1. Impure motives
2. Non-moral things.
3. A selfish desire to be free to act without regard for others.
4. Those who would bind their scruples on us.
(First published in FIRM FOUNDATION, Feb. 7, 1961)

Chapter 8

GOSPEL AND DOCTRINE

Although we garnish the tomb of Alexander Campbell, if he were here today, he would be unwelcome in most pulpits of the Church of Christ. Certainly, the guardians of the faith would denounce him for this statement:

"There was teaching, there was singing, there was praying, there was exhortation in the Christian church, but preaching in the church or to the church is not once mentioned in the Christian scriptures!

"Paul once, in his first letter to the church in Corinth, said he would declare to the Corinthians that gospel which he had preached to them, which also they had received and wherein they stood. We preach, or report, or proclaim news. But who teaches news? Who exhorts news? We preach the gospel to unbelievers, to aliens, but never to Christians, or those who have received it." (Millenial Harbinger, April 1862; copied from THE TWISTED SCRIPTURES, p. 43, by Carl Ketcherside; other thoughts are adapted from that source also.)

The revealed word of God in the New Testament writings contains two kinds of messages to accomplish two different purposes. Campbell recognized this, but that distinction has been obscured to most of us in this century. That lack of understanding has added to our confusion and led us away from any practical basis for unity among those in Christ. If the entire New Testament is the gospel, since a person must know, believe, and obey the gospel in order to be saved, one must know, believe, and obey everything in the New Testament to be saved. Every point of teaching becomes a life-or-death matter. Belief in any error would be damning. If all are not in exact conformity, then someone is lost.

So, in view of our list of differences in Chapter One, it looks hopeless for all of us, for who can be sure that he knows, believes, understands, and obeys all that is taught in the word of God? For example, such instructions as, "Grieve not the Holy Spirit of God" (Eph. 4:30), "Be filled with the Spirit" (Eph. 5:18), and "Pray in the Holy Spirit" (Jude 30) become frightening, for I don't really know whether I am understanding and doing those things or not.

Then too, if I can know and obey all, I don't need grace; hence, I would make void the grace of Christ by my law keeping.

Although these two kinds of messages are not isolated into different paragraphs, books, or epistles, there is a valid distinction to be made. There is the gospel which brings us into life and the teachings which direct our lives. The gospel gets us on the life raft and the Apostolic teachings guide us on to ultimate rescue. The gospel gets us on the Lord's work force and the doctrine directs our work on the job. The gospel brings us into fellowship while the doctrine/teaching guides those in fellowship.

The gospel is the good news, but, as Campbell asks, who teaches good news? The gospel was fully preached on Pentecost but all the epistles came later. The gospel was preached — heralded, proclaimed, evangelized — while the doctrine was imparted by teaching, instruction, reproof, rebuke, and exhortation. The gospel message was conveyed through evangelists, but prophets, pastors, and teachers edified through teaching.

The gospel is "the faith" which was already delivered (Jude 3), to which they were obedient (Acts 6:7), which Elymas resisted (Acts 13:8), in which the disciples should continue (Acts 14:22), which was the basis of unity (Eph. 4:13). The faith is the basis of our salvation.

Differences of understanding and conviction about the teachings were matters of faith. Romans 14 deals with this point. One man had faith to eat all things while another was weak in faith with scruples (v. 1-2). The faith (convictions) you have keep between yourself and God (v. 22). One who violates his scruples or convictions does not act from faith; hence, he sins (v. 23).

Paul epitomizes the gospel as the death, burial, and resurrection (1 Cor. 15:3). In a fuller definition, the gospel is the good news of the Sonship of Jesus, His atonement, His resurrection, His glorification, His return to raise the dead. One cannot deny any element of this and be saved for that would be a denial of the saving role of Jesus, not just a denial of facts. Facts have no saving power.

The gospel was not preached to the church. There is no record of such, no instruction for it, and no need for it. Although the word "preach" is used over one hundred times in the New Testament writings, it is not used in reference to a believing assembly. It is the word for "evangelize." The message was the gospel, the good news, the "evangel" while the one who proclaimed it was the preacher, the evangelist.

Other verbs relate to the edification of the saints. For example, in First Corinthians 14, there are fifty uses of verbs of communication in the assembly, such as speak, prophesy, utter, interpret, instruct, teach, declare, pray, sing, bless, and say, but preach or evangelize is not used. Revelation, knowledge, prophesy, and teaching are mentioned, but not preaching.

Paul wrote that "prophecy is not for unbelievers but for believers" (1 Cor. 14:22). "When you come together," he instructs, "Let all things be done for edification" (v. 26). In verse 4 he states, "He who prophesies edifies the church." Tongue speaking required interpreters "so that the church may be edified" (v. 5). So prophesy was for the believers and preaching was for the unbelievers.

Objectors to this distinction refer to various passages which are supposed to refute it. Let us consider them concisely.

Acts 20:7: Here it is written that Paul preached to the church at Troas. The word preached here as it is used in the King James Version is from the root word for dialogue, not evangelize or proclaim. "Paul talked with them" is rightly translated in the Revised Standard Version.

Romans 1:7: It is pointed out that this epistle was written to disciples and that Paul was eager to preach the gospel to them (1:15). Both MacKnight and Coffman agree that "to all that are in Rome" includes unbelieving Jews and Gentiles.

Romans 1:15: MacKnight, Coffman, and Batey (Living Word) agree that "you that are in Rome" is not restricted to disciples.

Romans 2:1-29 reveals that, although this epistle was written to the believers primarily, Paul also addressed some of it to unbelievers. Every Restoration commentator whose works are at hand agrees that Romans 2 is directed to unbelieving Jews. Undoubtedly, this chapter is addressed to, not just about, the unbelieving Jews in Rome. These Paul would seek to evangelize, desiring to "reap some harvest among you as well as among the rest of the Gentiles" (1:13). Chapter 15;8-24 is a context for this.

1 Corinthians 15:1-2: Paul had preached the gospel to those in Corinth. He was the one who evangelized them, but it is absurd to contend that he continued that activity to those who were converted.

2 Thessalonians 1:7-9: It is contended that this passage teaches that the Christian will be lost if he rejects the gospel, but the passage says nothing about a Christian rejecting it. Those who obey not the gospel will be lost. The Christian has already obeyed it.

Matthew 28:18-20: Rather than denying the distinction between the gospel and the teachings, a proper rendering as in the RSV supports the distinction. It says to "make disciples of all nations . . . teaching them to observe . . . " The non-Christian is not condemned for not keeping the doctrine for it was not addressed to him. He will be lost, however, if he rejects the gospel which is addressed to him.

It is through the gospel that salvation was brought. Nothing has been added to it since Pentecost. Paul "fully preached the gospel of Christ" from Jerusalem to Illyricum before Romans was written. Romans and the prison epistles could not have been a part of it. Nor were the writings of John. The unchanging gospel had already been preached when Paul wrote to the Galatians (Gal. 1:6-9).

This gospel message of "the faith" was "once for all delivered to the saints" (Jude 3) before Jude was written, so it could not have included Jude. People were "obedient to the faith" (Acts 6:7) before any epistle was written. Peter speaks of persons "having been begotten again through the word of God" (1 Peter 1:23), then he identifies the element of the word which begot as "the word of good tidings which was preached unto you" (1:25). It was the gospel/evangel preached/evangelized.

If all of the New Testament writings are the gospel, then a sinner could not be saved without being taught it in its entirety, for he must believe the gospel before he can be saved (Mark 16:15f). He still would be unsaved until he obeyed all that is enjoined in the other writings. Thus, the quick conversion of those on Pentecost, the Ethiopian eunuch, and the jailor could not have been accomplished for a thorough course of indoctrination would have been necessary first. And who ever learns and obeys all the teachings even in many years of sincere effort?

New creatures in Christ who are saved and in fellowship must be fed, confirmed, and matured so they will continue in fellowship and salvation. From the point of spiritual birth there will be diversity in disciples in knowledge, understanding, strength, ability, and maturity. Their justification is in being made right by an act of grace, not because they are right in all things. They are in the right because they are in Christ who is their righteousness, though they may not be right in all matters of faith. They are walking in the light, continually cleansed, and in fellowship (1 John 1:5-10). There is unity in the faith but diversity in matters of faith. Fellowship is not destroyed by failure to understand all the scriptures and to hold the perfect interpretation of them. But the believer must "long for the spiritual milk . . . that you may grow" (1 Peter 2:2), mature to eat solid food (Heb. 5:12f), and continue in the apostles' teaching (Acts 2:42).

Fellowship is established when that element of the word called "the gospel" is believed and obeyed. Fellowship is sustained with God and man by following the other "teachings" of the word. []

CHAPTER 9

OUR CREED

Throughout my career as a preacher, I have denounced denominational creeds. I could always explain happily, "We have no creed but Christ; when Peter confessed that Jesus is the Christ, he confessed the only creed upon which the church is built. That is the one foundation of the church. We ask a penitent sinner no question other than that which was asked the Ethiopian treasurer."

That is good and true and right. Christ is the foundation of our relationship with God and His people. The church is built upon the rock/fact that Jesus is the Christ. However, let that convert come out of the water of baptism and the creed that I would impose upon him was suddenly expanded to include all my interpretations and convictions about the teachings in the New Testament scriptures. By giving him some time to mature to my doctrinal positions, I could tolerate his disagreement on some things, but if he continued to go against my real doctrinal hangups, my coolness toward him might discourage him to the point that he would leave the fellowship. Then I would be off the hook and could use him as an example of apostasy because of error, concluding that he was never really converted to the Church of Christ anyway. But in reality he was simply refusing to accept my sectarian creed and stance.

Does not the preceding speak of us generally?

A person's fellowship and salvation in Christ is accomplished through his becoming "obedient to the faith" (Acts 6-7). One must believe the message about Christ (Mark 16:15f). That "Jesus is the Christ" becomes his confessed creed (Acts 8:37). That belief in Jesus must cause one to determine to abandon sin and do His will (Acts 2:38). In response to his faith and in compliance with his repentance, one must be baptized. At this point one is saved, free from guilt, in Christ, a newborn creature, added to the one body which is the church.

That person is now in fellowship with Christ and with every other person who has followed that procedure and has not forfeited his fellowship later. This is that unity which is accomplished by the Spirit: "For by one Spirit we were all baptized into one body" (1 Cor. 12:13).

In reaching this state that person was asked no question except, "Do you believe that Jesus is the Christ, the Son of God?" No inquiry was made of his convictions or practices relating to eating meats, the use of God's name as a by-word, present day demon possession and exorcism, praying for healing, killing in self-defense, midweek communion, or any other of the many issues listed in Chapter One which may relate to his faithful practice of the Christian life. Do convictions and practices of such issues matter? Some, like days and meats (Romans 14) and circumcision (Gal. 5:6), do not. Some may be sinful, though their status is debated by sincere and studious disciples. Different convictions on debatable issues can be held without disrupting fellowship. Such issues were not the basis on which the convert was saved or brought into fellowship.

Not the Creed

In the cases of conversion narrated in Acts, none of the prospects was given a course of indoctrination previous to baptism into Christ. So far as we know, none even was told before baptism that they would be made a part of the church with whom they would be expected to assemble, give, commune, and sing. In fact, though baptism was required of each, no lesson on the need and meaning of baptism was explained to them. The only explanation of the meaning of baptism was made much later to disciples, not to prospects (Rom. 6:1-11; Col. 2:11-14). Beliefs about these things were not a part of the creed.

From the time of being initiated into the one body through baptism forward, the converts will differ in knowledge, understanding, and convictions. Although they will continue to grow toward maturity, none will ever know and understand all. The most mature will still disagree on various issues such as listed in Chapter One.

Such differences are no serious problem except for the legalist who must be right in all points in order to live up to his own creed. There was great difference of conviction over circumcision in the early church; however, circumcision was neither a plus nor a minus unless it hindered their faithful, loving work (Gal. 5:6).

Many times I have stressed that, when two people disagree on something, one may be right and the other wrong, or they may both be wrong, but both certainly cannot be right. But how wrong I was! Legally, both could not be right. I was a legalist. Paul said that believers may disagree on meats and days and both be right for God welcomes and upholds both and makes both to stand (Rom. 14:1-4).

Paul calls upon disagreeing parties to accept and respect each other. The meat eater must not despise, disdain, or look down his nose at the scrupulous vegetarian and the vegetarian must not condemn the meat eater. We have not learned that lesson yet, for the conservative brother condemns the more liberal brother and, although the liberal does not condemn the conservative, he looks condescendingly and impatiently upon him. If this spirit prevails, then both are wrong, not because of differing convictions, but for lack of love and respect for each other as brothers.

Paul tantalizes the legalist by not telling which side was right on the matter of eating foods and keeping days. Instead, he shames us, "Who are you to pass judgment on the servant of another? It is before his own master that he stands or falls. And he will be upheld, for the Master is able to make him stand." On both sides of the issues, people were serving and honoring the Lord sincerely. Let the Lord accept or reject. "Why do you pass judgment on your brother? Or you, why do you despise your brother? Each of us shall give account of himself to God" (Rom. 14:10f). Fellowship must not be endangered by efforts to decide or bind scruples (Rom. 14:1).

This plea is continued into Romans 15 with Paul exhorting prayerfully, "May the God of steadfastness and encouragement grant you to live in such harmony with one another, in accord with Christ Jesus, that together you may with one voice glorify the God and Father of our Lord Jesus Christ" (15:5f). His following plea should have long since drained our pride and exclusiveness out of us: "Welcome one another, therefore, as Christ has welcomed you, for the glory of God" (15:7). How did He welcome me? When I was ugly, unloving, ignorant, misunderstanding, immature, and a sinner! He accepted me on my faith in Him who is my righteousness when I obeyed the gospel, not because I was such a nice, loving, righteous, correct, and knowledgeable person. As He accepted and continues to accept me, so I am to accept you. Being accepted, who am I to reject others? Yea, how dare I reject others?

Some have been heard to say, "The New Testament is our only creed." Many, though not saying it, accept the epistles as an extension of the creed, making knowledge, belief, and understanding of each part necessary. This makes doctrinal correctness the basis of unity, and by doctrinal correctness, we mean, "Conform to my interpretation, my creed, and we will all be united!" But that is unreal. It makes unity an illusive phantom. "Be like us!" Which group of us? We will ever be divided by a doctrinal approach to unity, for it allows for no diversity.

If the above is true, why are we warned against false teachers? Good question! But please hold it for the next chapter.

Jesus is the Creed

Our belief is not in efficacious tenents of faith which we call the gospel — belief in the Sonship, atonement, resurrection, and ascension. These have no saving power though it is declared that the gospel is God's power to save (Rom. 1:16). The power is in Christ who is the Good News of salvation. But deny any of these facts and you destroy the creed because you have taken away the basis of hope in Christ. He that believes not shall be damned.

The Gnostics in apostolic times denied that Jesus came in the flesh. To deny the incarnation was to fail to abide in the doctrine of Christ on which the gospel rested. "Anyone who goes ahead and does not abide in the doctrine of Christ does not have God; he who abides in the doctrine has both the Father and the Son" (2 John 9). This was said of "men who will not acknowledge the coming of Jesus Christ in the flesh" (v.7). That was not referring to instrumental music or kitchens in church buildings, but to our creed, Jesus Christ.

That which destroys the faith as the Gnostic teaching was doing destroys the basis of salvation. Teachers of such were not to be welcomed or encouraged (2 John 10) but were to be delivered to Satan (1 Tim. 1:19f; 2 Tim. 2:18f).

A person turning to Jesus must repent, dedicating himself to moral living. Some may willfully abandon this purity of life while still holding to the faith. That is an incompatable situation. The flagrantly immoral must be delivered to Satan also (1 Cor. 5). The sincerely ignorant, weak, or stumbling disciple is not in that category, however.

Since we are all baptized into one body, a divisive person cannot be tolerated. So Paul instructs, "As for a man who is factious, after admonishing him once or twice, have nothing more to do with him, knowing that such a person is perverted and sinful; he is self condemned" (Titus 3:10f). Not all who disagree or teach some error are factional. Persons could disagree on circumcision, meats, and days and still be in harmony in the one body. A factious person solicits adherents, builds a party, and causes division. He can do this without teaching. Most factions are over personalities and power struggles, but they usually choose some issue as a white horse to ride out on as a way of saving face.

Agreement on all teachings is not the basis of unity for we could never have practical unity in even one small congregation. No one should be subjected to the credal pronouncements of the preacher or elders. A sincere belief which differs from that of the "powers that be" in the congregation is no just cause for withdrawal of fellowship. If a person becomes factional, however, by forcing his scruple on others, that would be another matter and it should be dealt with.

About forty years ago I heard of a man who wished to become a Baptist preacher. Upon completion of his training, he sought to be ordained. In the ordination procedure, he was asked if he would agree to preach Baptist doctrine. He replied that he would just preach the Bible. They pressed the question and he stood by his answer. Consequently, he was not ordained!

For many years I took delight in relating that story to contrast our lack of a church creed. We just preach the Bible. But I use that story no more since becoming honest enough with myself to admit that I cannot always just preach the Bible and be permitted to remain in the pulpit. I must conform to the party line, the unwritten creed, of the church or I will be dismissed and my family will be without income. If I teach the wrong truths from the Bible, I am branded as a troublemaker and even other churches are warned of me. I know! One must conform to the creed!

A Questionnaire

Also, elders began to require that prospective teachers fill out and sign a questionnaire — not a creed, mind you, just a questionnaire! These questionnaires usually do not require much of a positive spiritual nature; rather they are expressions of the credal hangups of the elders, such as divorce, smoking, drinking, and dancing — especially dancing! Wonder why they don't include speeding on the highway? For each dancer we have a caravan of speeders. But the elders have no hangup about speeding because they speed. That's not in their creed — oops, questionnaire!

When given this questionnaire, suppose that the prospective teacher should simply write, "I will just teach the Bible," and return it. Would that person be assigned a class? That's another reason why I don't talk much about Baptist creeds any more.

If a person holds a belief in conflict with mine, I have a right to discuss it and study with him about it. It becomes impelling to do so if I consider it to be soul-threatening. All the time, however, I must love and respect him and refrain from judging him. "Who are you to judge the servant of another?" Because I am his brother in fellowship in Christ does not mean that I sanction or approve all he teaches or does, but it should, yea must, mean that I do not judge him or force him to conform to my scruples. "The faith that you have, keep between yourself and God" (Rom. 14:22). Although I disapprove of his actions, he cannot violate my conscience. Only I can do that.

When a person asks to be a part of the congregation in which I am a part, neither I, the elders, nor the congregation has any right to ask him more than, "Have you been baptized into Christ; do you strive to live a life of holiness, and do you seek

-62-

to live in harmony with God's people?" That will cover the basis of original initiation into the body and its continuing fellowship and unity. To ask if he has been a member of the Church of Christ elsewhere, or to write to his previous congregation to get the low-down on him, is both judgmental and sectarian.

How would we know the applicant was not formerly associated with the Christian Church or the Assembly of God? We wouldn't. Would it contaminate us to serve with someone in Christ who wore some sectarian name other than ours? We have no alternative other than to accept him. It is not our prerogative to judge him. He answers to God just as we do. Why should it be harder to accept him than all the others in the congregation who disagree on the hundred issues in Chapter One? And why can't I accept him as a brother while he is still serving in the Christian Church or the Assembly of God with no thought of joining our congregation?

Why do we feel so much more comfortable in rejecting others than in receiving them? I would prefer to stand before God in judgment having received someone whom God had rejected than to have to give account for rejecting one whom God had accepted. It is a deadly spiritual disease of sectarian spirit that motivates one to reject one whom God has received, condemning brothers whom God forbad us to judge.

Why do I make such a point of this? Have I just developed a rebellious spirit? It is because I can no longer stand to see the church sectarianized. When an individual judges others and binds his scruples, he becomes factious. When a group binds its scruples and measures others by them, it becomes sectarian. Even though it may be unwritten, a creed creates and protects an exclusive sect. It excludes others who will not conform, though they be brothers. That makes the group a sect. To name is to denominate. When the group gives itself a distinguishing name, it then becomes a sectarian denomination. Can you deny that the Church of Christ has reached that state?

Those who are free in Christ stand free from the creeds and judgements of men.

Chapter 10

FALSE TEACHERS

In promoting and defending our doctrinal positions, we preachers have made many denunciations of false teachers whom we identified as persons who teach error. While we have admitted that no one teaches total error, we have declared that any point of error is sufficient to pervert the word of God and to make its proponent a false teacher.

Such branding has a solid, fundamental ring to it until one inquires a bit more deeply. The denouncer implies that he himself is in error on no point! He is right on everything; hence, he is no false teacher. Others teach some error, so they are false teachers. How blind and bigoted can one become!

Warning us of the gravity of becoming teachers, James assures us, "For we all make many mistakes, and if any one makes not mistakes in what he says he is a perfect man ... " (James 3:2f). So, if teaching some error makes one a false teacher, all are false teachers.

It may be surprising to some to learn that the much-used term "false teacher" is used only once in the New Testament writings (2 Peter 2:1). The often heard companion expression "false teaching" is not found even once. False prophets and error are mentioned with some frequence.

The adjective "false" describes the man rather than his teaching. He is a teacher or prophet with a character defect which motivates him evilly rather than being a sincere teacher who is misinformed and holds a different conviction on some point or points. Let us review a few references to see that this is true.

1. The teachers whom Peter wrote about were insidious, greedy, licentious, exploiting, divisive, and God denying (2 Peter 2:1-3). They were not sincere, humble men who were ignorant or misunderstanding.

2. A factious man, because of his self-seeking ambition, is "perverted and sinful" (Titus 3:10f).

3. Persons departing from the faith would be "giving heed to deceitful spirits and doctrines of demons, through the pretensions of liars whose consciences are seared" (1 Tim. 4:1f). These were not honest men who had missed the point on some doctrinal issues. Evidently, these were the false prophets of 1 John 4:1-3, the Gnostics who denied that Jesus had come in the flesh, the antichrists, whose deceit and licentiousness John deals with throughout his three epistles.

4. "Men of corrupt mind and counterfeit faith," these insidious men were not simply persons ignorant of truth on certain points (2 Tim. 3:1-7). They were unscrupulous characters.

5. Paul dealt with many doctrinal problems in the Corinthian church with firm patience without demanding withdrawal from anyone on doctrinal grounds. Only the flagrantly impenitent immoral were to be excluded from their company. However, he unmasked those who were leading the dividing parties, declaring, "For such men are false apostles, deceitful workmen, disguising themselves as apostles of Christ" (2 Cor. 11:12f). It is not their doctrinal stance that is objectionable, but their corrupt character. Evidently these were the persons leading the dissensions who are rebuked in 1 Corinthians 1:10-15. Instead of being united in mind and judgment "that there be no dissensions among you" and all saying, "I am of Christ," they let selfish ambition lead to a splintering of the fellowship.

6. In Romans 14 and 15, Paul taught the saints to love and respect each other and to live in harmony even though they had some differing convictions. Those who disagreed were not to judge each other. They were not false teachers to be driven out. However, some, in opposition to what Paul had taught about living in harmony, were creating dissensions and difficulties, serving not "our Lord Christ, but their own appetites, and by fair and flattering words they deceive the hearts of the simple-minded" (Romans 16:17f). How we have misapplied this passage to justify division over doctrinal issues and quibbles.

These selfish deceivers were not identified in the Roman epistle. Later, Paul wrote of the problem there while he was imprisoned in Rome. He declared, "Some indeed preach Christ from envy and rivalry, but others from good will. The latter do it out of love, knowing that I am put here for the defense of the gospel; the former proclaim Christ out of partisanship, not sincerely but thinking to afflict me in my imprisonment. What then? Only that in every way, whether in pretense or in truth, Christ is proclaimed; and in that I rejoice" (Phil. 1:15-18). These men were preaching Christ, but they were also preaching circumcision and making it a dividing issue. Paul identifies them as such in Philippiams 3:2-11. Then he reveals their true character: "For many, of whom I have often told you and now tell you even with tears, live as enemies of the cross of Christ. Their end is destruction, their god is the belly, and they glory in their shame, with minds set on earthly things" (3:18f). They were materialistic, earthly minded, self-serving men using the immaterial doctrinal issue of circumcision as a tool to divide.

No such denunciation is made of the contenders for circumsision involved in the Jerusalem conference in Acts 15.The quality of the men was different, except for the false brethren who slipped in to spy at Antioch (Gal. 2:4). They were not false men even though they had a different conviction about circumcision.

We are in error when we castigate someone who differs from us in his sincere effort to know and do the will of God. He is doing all that you or I can do — his best. He is in error on some things even as you and I are in error on some things. The only brothers we have are brothers in error, someone had observed.

Neither side at the Jerusalem conference were false prophets; nor was the sincere Apollos, who was in error on a major doctrine through lack of information. Great teachers and reformers of the past, though they may never have gained some necessary doctrinal understandings, cannot be denounced as false teachers. They were honest searchers even, as I trust you and I are. We have profited from their search. We can see further by standing on their shoulders. Thank God for them!

Jesus warned, "Beware of false prophets, who come to you in sheep's clothing but inwardly are ravenous wolves. You will know them by their fruits. Are grapes gathered from thorns, or figs from thistles?" (Matt. 7:15f). We have been inclined to interpret that as "by their teachings you shall know them," but Jesus declares that the fruit of life will reveal the truth or falsity of the character.

Do we gain our confidence and satisfaction from contrasting our teachings with the teachings of those we denounce, or are we willing to compare the fruits of our lives with those of the people whom we oppose doctrinally? My self-esteem begins to shrink when I make such a comparison. The character of the teacher determines the kind of fruit that will be forthcoming. Many defenders of doctrine have, because of defective character and motive, produced the most unholy fruit of division and have been guilty of destroying God's holy temple (1 Cor. 3:16f).

Jesus said, ". . . no one who does a mighty work in my name will be able soon after to speak evil of me. For he that is not against us is for us" (Mark 9:39f).

The foregoing conclusions have not been reached easily, for I, too, long denounced as false teachers those who teach differently from me.

Those who have gained freedom in Christ are free to accept brothers who bear the fruit of the Spirit even though they are not in total doctrinal agreement.

Chapter 11

WHY SHOULD WE DENOMINATE OURSELVES?

When the Lord adds the saved to His church, He does not make them parts of a sect or denomination. They are the church. As there is only one church, it needs no name. God gave it none. He did not denominate it. To name is to denominate; to denominate is to name. A denomination is a class or kind having a specific name. To give the church a name is to give it a denominational trait.

A proper name designates a specific person, place, or thing like John Doe; Rochester, Texas; or Congress. Proper names should be capitalized. "Man" is a common or class name distinguishing us from animals, trees, cars, and metals. Generally we can be designated as persons, individuals, inhabitants, and homo sapiens. We may be described as intelligent, moral, passionate, and inventive. None of these designations or descriptions are the proper name of man either individually or collectively.

In like manner the term "church" distinguishes the saved from lodges, banks, corporations, and labor unions. Other designations, such as body, kingdom, and family, reveal its nature. None of these, however, is a proper name for the saved people.

Names are given to identify. A person wishes to be distinguished from all other persons. So he accepts a specific, or proper name. His name may be Hook. There are other Hooks. So he accepts a full proper name of Solomon Slaughter Hook. That distinguishes him from everybody else! (That was my father's name).

The church, being one, needs no proper name to identify it as being different. Sects and divisions may want to identify themselves because of their lack of identity with the one church. So they name (denominate) themselves. When we denominate ourselves, how can we convince others that we are not really a denomination?

If the Lord had intended that the body of believers have a proper name, surely He would have told us about it. But He didn't. The claim that church of God, church of the living God, church of the first-born, church of Christ, and church of the saints are all proper names is unfounded and confusing. Since no proper name is given for the church, who can claim that one name is more authentic or scriptural than another?

Some seek to solve the name problem by referring to the body as the church of Christ with a little "c". It is true that the word "church" is not capitalized in scriptural usage; however, it is not used as a proper noun in the Scriptures. Putting "church of Christ" on the sign, letterhead, and bulletin violates basic grammar. "church of Christ" is being used as a proper name, and proper names must be capitalized.

An acceptance of the name "Church of Christ" has been nurtured which is sectarian in spirit. The name has come to have a true ring to it. We hear about Church of Christ preachers, Church of Christ literature, Church of Christ colleges, and Church of Christ weddings. In publications we read of congregations being specified as Northside Church of Christ, Eastside Church of Christ, and Westside Church of Christ. Isn't it sufficient to use Northside church, or, if that is the full and accepted name of the group, Northside Church? Individual congregations may be designated rightly by location without any sectarian name.

Evidently Paul was in the church of God at Corinth when he wrote: "the churches of Christ salute you." In sending greetings from the church of God of Corinth, was he sending greetings from a church of Christ or from a Church of Christ?

Techniques of scholasticism have been employed to support loyalty to the name "Church of Christ." These devised arguments maintain that (1) the church belongs to Christ; hence it should wear his name, and (2) the church is the bride of Christ, and a bride always honors the husband by wearing his name.

The church does belong to Christ, but which inspired writer used that as an argument for a proper name? How far does that rule apply? My dog belongs to me, but it does not wear my name. The church belongs to God also. How does the rule apply here? Which of our buildings has "Church of God" on it?

If the church wears the Savior's name, it will be called the "church of Jesus" because His name was Jesus, not Christ.

My bride honored me by wearing my name, but we have no record in the Bible of any wife wearing her husband's name. We have taken a modern Western custom and tried to make a Biblical pattern out of it. Wives still do not wear their husbands' names in some countries and cultures today.

To argue that the bride should wear the name of the groom is to admit that the church should have a proper name to denominate it.

My wife wears my name, but she did not do so until after our marriage. Jesus and His bride are engaged, but not married. His bride has not been presented to Him yet (Ephesians 5:25-28). We have been invited to their wedding (Revelation 19:7-9; 21:2).

If the body of the saved is to have a proper title, we are still faced with a problem. The Greek word from which "church" is derived is not even used in the New Testament in relation to God's people! When you look up the word "church" in *An Expository Dictionary of New Testament Words* by Vine, you will be instructed to see "assembly" and "congregation". There is no listing under the word "church".

The Greek word "ecclesia" has been translated into the English word "church", but that is not its meaning. The word "church" is derived from the Greek word "kuriakos". You may learn that from your English dictionary. That word is used only in 1 Corinthians 11:20 and Revelation 1:10, and it means: belonging to the Lord; pertaining to the Lord. How could a word which has no counterpart in the New Testament be a part of an authorized title for God's people?

The Greek word "ecclesia", in pre-Christian use, designated a regular assembly of the whole body of citizens in a free city-state called out by the heralds for the discussion and decision of public business. Jesus took this common word to describe those whom He would save. The emphasis is not on what or where they were called out from, but in being called into an assembly. The closest single-word translation into English would be assembly or congregation.

Assemblies designated by location may be parts of the general assembly and church of the first-born ones. We have ample scriptural precedent for designating congregations by location. They had no problem about identity in the first century. We have a denominational problem today. Why add to the problem by denominating ourselves? Let those who wish to be distinguished from the universal church take distinctive names. But if we are a part of the universal church, why should we want to be distinguished from it?

Time honored names are not changed readily. It is hard for us to admit a need for change. It is painful to change from that to which we have become accustomed. Reform never comes easily. It has never been the easiest course to speak where the Bible speaks and to call Bible things by Bible names.

Chapter 12

FREE FROM SECTARIANISM

While living in the friendly little city of Lovington, New Mexico a few years ago, I developed a relaxed friendship with L. S. "Manny" Loveall, a minister of the Christian Church there. Manny and I were able to discuss matters rather objectively without each feeling that he was bound to protect his party allegiance.

I noticed that Manny had a set of Jule Miller filmstrips like the ones that I used at times to teach a prospect. As we compared our teaching and methods, we learned that we each baptized persons in order that they might receive the remission of sins upon the prerequisite of confession of faith in Christ and repentance of sins. We each taught the prospect that he would be baptized into Christ, into the one body which is the church which is not a denomination. We would explain that this would make him simply a Christian. We agreed that teaching on issues like the use of instrumental music were not a part of the conversion process.

Then we mused about the preplexing result of our similar actions. When he baptized a person into Christ and His church, it automatically made that person a member of the Christian Church. When I baptized a person into Christ and His church, it automatically made that person a member of the Church of Christ. The process was the same in both cases. What, then, made the difference in the results? Why would one of us produce the Church of Christ and the other produce the Christian Church?

One possible explanation would be that the person who did the baptizing made the difference. But how could that be? The convert's salvation was based on his own belief and obedience, not that of the baptizer. And it is the Lord who does the adding, not the preacher.

Another answer — and the correct one — is that the Lord did not add these converts to the Church of Christ and/or the Christian Church. He added them to His one church. The Spirit directed their baptism into the one body (1 Cor. 12:13). There is only one.

When these converts chose to be in the fellowship with the Christian Church or the Church of Christ, they chose to be a part of a sect. In these two groups persons have all been baptized into the one body, the church. Then they distinguish themselves from the one body and from one another by wearing distinguishing names. To name is to denominate; to denominate is to name. The Lord gave no name for His church. Now, they have become sectarian denominations! Each group is a part of the whole church but not in fellowship with the whole. They are sectarian divisions.

My brothers in Christ, what other answer can you put forth? This answer has not come to me easily. It is born of pain — in the anguish of facing disturbing truth with complete intellectual honesty.

Perhaps you hold to the objection that the Church of Christ has a scriptural name and the Christian Church doesn't. That's an evasion. The difference in those names is less than the difference in tweedle-dee and tweedle-dum. One is the Church "of Christ" and the other is the "of Christ" Church.

The real point is that they are distinguishing, exclusive names, and God did not intend that we distinguish and He gave us no distinguishing name.

These two groups do not have to merge into one congregation. They should each designate themselves simply as the church and, as such, they should rejoice that they are in fellowship in Christ. They have differing scruples, but neither judges or disdains the other any longer. They are one body but two congregations. It is not the meeting in one congregation nor having identical convictions that make them one. It is being in Christ that makes them one. Churches are not in or out of fellowship with each other. That is an individual relationship accomplished when we are baptized into Christ, whether baptized by Manny Loveall, Cecil Hook, or any other sectarian.

To be free in Christ, we must be free of sectarian spirit and practice.

Chapter 13

SECTARIAN BAPTISM

After fifty years of observation in the Church of Christ as both a listener and a preacher, I am forced to admit that we have emphasized baptism above all other points of teaching. Hardly a lesson comes from our pulpits that does not mention baptism and it has been the theme of countless other lessons.

Baptism is a necessary part of our obedience. Can we overemphasize that which is necessary? Yes. Vitamin C is necessary to our physical health but, if we make it our chief claim to health, then things are out of proportion and health can be lost. So it is with baptism or any other overstressed doctrine or practice. Overemphasis of baptism puts us out of balance, develops into a creedal test, and becomes a sectarian device. Because our teachings on baptism have seemed so solidly scriptural, it has been no easy matter for me to arrive at this conclusion.

By the Catholic theologians who have developed the sacramental system, a sacrament is defined as a visible rite or ceremony instituted by Christ to give grace. The scriptures give no such designation, definition, or description. Yet most of us have accepted that concept of baptism — that it is a ceremony by which grace is conferred upon us. Thus, though denying it, we have accepted the concept of baptismal regeneration.

Baptism symbolizes the change that an individual has undergone. He has changed from unbelief to trust in Jesus. He has determined to cease his sinful life and to seek to live a holy life. Instead of being guilty any longer, he is now pronounced innocent by his proxy, Jesus. He is like Noah, who being a righteous man, had his righteousness confirmed when the waters separated him from the rest of the world. He is like the Israelites who, after a long process of separation, had their freedom confirmed by the Red Sea. The seed of the word con-

ceives in his heart, spiritual life is initiated, and then he is
brought forth symbolically by the confirming act of baptism.
Life and salvation are not conferred by a sacrament, but the
process of becoming a saved person is symbolized and confirmed
by the action of baptism.

Baptism is symbolic of the whole change of the sinner into
a new creature in Christ. It becomes as a metonymy, a literary
device where the part is used to represent the whole. Belief is
for the remission of sins. Confession is for the remission of sins.
Repentance is for the remission of sins. Baptism is for the remission of sins. All of these combine in the whole process toward
obtaining forgiveness. When a person is baptized, it must mean
that all these other conditions have been accomplished. When
baptism is said to save us, a part of the conversion process is
used to represent the whole with baptism being the finalizing
act.

The Purpose of Baptism

We have stressed that a person must be baptized purposely
for the remission of sins for his baptism to be valid. Do we ever
question a person like this: "Did you believe purposely for the
remission of sins? When you repented, did you have in mind
that the purpose was for the remission of sins? Did you understand that you were confessing for the remission of sins? If you
are not sure that you did those things purposely for the remission of sins, then you must re-believe, re-confess, and re-repent
for the right purposes"? Why do we just pick on baptism? Is it
because it is more sacramental to the receiving of grace than
the other actions? You know, a sacrament must be performed
exactly right for its mystical qualities to work!

I have never heard of one of us preachers trying to stir up
doubts and guilt by asking, "Were you baptized purposely in
order to receive the gift of the Holy Spirit?" We have continued
to have lack of understanding and many misunderstandings
about the gift of the Holy Spirit. Yet I have heard of no one
demanding, "You must be re-baptized with the understanding
that it is in order to receive the gift of the Holy Spirit." God
promised both remission of sins and the gift of the Holy Spirit
on the same conditions. Why demand re-baptism because of

misinformation of one and not the other? Could it be a sectarian hangup of ours?

In her eighties, Grannie is ordered by her doctor to take several kinds of medication. She gets confused about the purpose of the various pills. She may think the pill given to relieve her dizziness is the one to ease her arthritis. Will her confusion and misunderstanding make the pill ineffective in relieving her dizziness? She follows the orders of the doctor who understands. She has only to obey him. So when a penitent believer obeys his or her Lord, though that person may be confused as to when the Lord fulfills His promise, it will not cause the Lord to withhold the promised results. The faith is in Christ, not baptism. We may, ⊾nd do, misunderstand many things relating to our obedience in all areas but we are obeying Him who understands. We have only to obey sincerely.

Evidently the Roman disciples did not understand the full meaning of their own baptism experience, so Paul explained it to them. The only explanations about baptism in the scriptures were made to disciples rather than to candidates for baptism (Romans 6; Colossians 2). There is no record of a lesson explaining the meaning of baptism being delivered to persons in the conversion process. They were taught faith in the gospel about Christ and then told what to do in obeying Him. In Acts 2:38, "unto the remission of sins" was not a part of the commmand but a part of the results promised.

I am not evading the fact that some were re-baptized (Acts 18:24-28; 19:1-7). Those disciples at Ephesus had not been baptized in obedience to the command of Jesus in the Great Commission. The question Paul asked them was not, "Were you baptized for the forgiveness of sins?" But rather, "Did you receive the Holy Spirit when you believed?" In the recorded conversation, Paul did not explain the purpose of baptism. In their lacking of the Holy Spirit, Paul saw evidence that they had received John's baptism instead of that required by Jesus.

When a person is baptized, he is baptized into Christ, into the body, into the church, into the kingdom, into the family of God, etc. whether he understands all of that or not. Later, when he comes to understand all the purposes of baptism, he is not to be baptized again.

If the baptizer states the purpose in the ritual as being for the remission of sins, then doesn't that eliminate by silence the many other purposes — to be born again, to be in Christ, to put on Christ, to enter the body, etc.? To say the least, it puts a sectarian emphasis on the one point. The baptizer is only instructed to baptize into the name of the Father, the Son, and the Holy Spirit.

When you move into our community and "place your membership" — a good scriptural term! — I do not ask about your baptism before receiving you in the local fellowship. I do not know if, how, or why you were baptized. I receive you on your own profession. You accept me on mine. That is as it should be. Each man is to judge himself. If I consider you to be wrong, I can teach you but not judge you. We welcome fellowship with "outsiders" in all our activities in assemblies but refuse to accept them on the church roll. The non-scriptural "membership roll" is a hangup of ours.

We generally will not receive a person on his sectarian baptism, so we make him conform to our own sectarian baptism. However, the person who is baptized into Christ is baptized into Christ's church by the same process. If we conclude that baptism puts him in the Christian Church, the Baptist Church, the Church of Christ, or any other group distinguished from others by a name, we have become sectarian in concept and practice. It is not the baptism that is sectarian. Baptism is the Lord's. It is we who become sectarian in trying to appropriate baptism as a device to create a group distinguished from other baptized believers.

All who have been baptized into the Savior must drop these sectarian distinctions and recognize that we are brothers in the same Christ and His church. Thus breaking free from our sectarian cage, we are free to recognize millions of brothers and sisters in Christ whom we previously disdained, judged, and rejected. Let's let God do the judging. Let's do the loving.

"But they are brothers in error!" That's right. That's the only kind of brothers I have.

Chapter 14

PIE-SHAPED RELIGION

We have been building a lot of pie-shaped church buildings and trying to fill them with pie-shaped religion.

All of us have seen the sectional graphs used to shame us to greater activity. In them proportionate wedges show how much of our time or money we use for work, sleep, recreation, and such, and then there is the thin slice which is given in worship and service. That thin little wedge of pie is intended to represent our frail claim for righteousness

A similar illustration speaks of the six days God gives us for our personal use and the one day He gives for worship and service — which day many also appropriate for themselves, except for an hour or two or three. Another illustration reveals that God gives us 604,800 seconds each week which we appropriate generously to various necessary activities while we reserve only 3,600 seconds for worship and service to Him — only 1/168th of our time given to the Lord!

These illustrations imply that the only worship and service is formal, public, organized, and usually related to the assemblies. Attendance is usually the most visible expression of our religion, so it becomes the measuring stick of our religion. All the Christian qualities which reveal our character and rule our daily conduct run a poor second in importance to attendance.

Paul would have us to give the whole pie to God. "I appeal to you therefore, brethren, by the mercies of God, to present your bodies as a living sacrifice, holy and acceptable to God, which is your spiritual worship" (Rom. 12:1). Paul alludes to worship under the Law of Moses. Under that system, the worshipper selected—set apart, dedicated, made holy, consecrated, sanctified — the animal to be offered. At the specified time, the animal was taken to the tabernacle/temple where the Presence of God dwelt. There it was presented to the priest to be offered by him through the high priest in a specified, ritualistic manner. The priest inspected the animal to see that it was acceptable; then he took its life as an offering. An offering is a sacrifice. To sacrifice is to offer. This procedure was considered acceptable worship.

Our sacrifice is the offering of the whole self — the body and all that relates to it. It is set apart, commited, dedicated, made holy, sanctified in daily life rather than in a single dying act. This continuous offering is not taken to a priest or place at a certain time to fulfill ritualistic details. The sanctified one does not go to a priest, for he is a priest himself, offering himself through his High Priest. Worship and service does not take him to a temple, for he is a temple of the Presence of the Spirit. His service is not at set times with detailed rituals, for all of his life is an offering to God, totally sanctified. This becomes acceptable sacrifice, a continuous offering. Worship and service is all that goes on in the temple! All the activity in the Jewish temple was not ritual, but the work of the Levites in caring for the vessels, mopping the floor, or repairing was necessary part. The whole of the temple operation was a continuous offering even as, in a ritualistic way, the showbread and candles were a continuous, living sacrifice.

Although there are different shades of meaning in the different words used for worship, there is no clear distinction between worship and service. Some actions and thoughts are directed specifically to God (We have ritualized these into a "worship service"); some are directed to other people, and some are rendered toward self in the maintaining of the temple. When one's life is dedicated to God, whatever he does is worship/service. It is not a matter of "Take time to be holy," for he is holy. It is not a matter of "Lord, we come before Thee now," for we are in Him and his Spirit is in us constantly.Through our commitment as a disciple, we "continually offer up a sacrifice of praise to God, that is, the fruit of lips that acknowledge his name" (Heb. 13:15).

As long as one is living with Christ as Lord in his life, he is a whole-life offering in worship. This will include all the mundane, secular things that relate to life. Although he may be working at a job, mowing his lawn, vacationing with his family, or taking medicine, these are not selfish, earthly, materialistic goals. They are a part of the upkeep of the temple which is continually devoted to God in all of its purposes.

The segmented concept of worship/service makes some questions difficult to answer. If one hour of formal religion per week is not enough, will two, three, fifteen, or thirty be sufficient? Similar questions may be asked about the percentage of giving. If the size of the slice of the pie is determined, whose is the remainder? Is the rest holy? How could this picture whole-life, continuous offering?

Usually the wedge of the pie is made to relate to what has been defined as "the five items of worship" — singing, praying, teaching, giving, and communing (or "taking communion," as many say, as though communion is something you can eat or drink!). For many years, I accepted, taught, and defended this "five items of worship" concept. After all, anyone who "searched the scriptures" here and there could find pieces of this puzzling pattern to put together. And surely no one would be simple enough to include fasting, the love least, foot washing, lifting up holy hands, elders anointing the sick and praying for them, distributing to the needs of the saints, or the holy kiss (which is commanded five times!) as acts of worship!

We have defined and specified all the fine points of these five acts of worship feeling assured that the "All-Seeing Eye" watches intently to see that we tithe all the mint, dill, and licorice. We have made God a God of quibbles. The awesome wrath of the God of the universe may be so aroused by our singing while passing the cup, for instance, that He may damn the whole assembly to eternal hell! How did we ever develop such a theology?

Is a housewife worshipping God more acceptably while singing in an assembly than when expressing the same feeling while cooking dinner or while singing along with recorded spiritual songs? Is it worship to "lay by in store" to help the needy, but less so to help the poor yourself, or to work on the job so you will have resources to help the poor? Are adoring thoughts inspired by singing "How Great Thou Art" in assembly more worshipful than adoring thoughts inspired by viewing nature on a picnic? Are appreciative reflections on the atonement less worship when they come while lying awake in bed than those that come while participating in the Lord's Supper? The value is not in keeping details of a ritual precisely, but in what we think and express.

According to the system of sacraments developed by the Catholic Church, a sacrament is a visible rite or ceremony through which God's grace is supposed to be bestowed upon the worshipper. We have inherited too much of that concept, assuming that special grace is dispensed through our acts of worship, if we keep all the specified details of the rituals. Actions of worship do not draw down God's grace or achieve justification. We don't worship to be justified but because we have been made righteous by His gift. What we do in our assemblies, as well as in the daily consecrated life, is to gain strength and to impart strength to others. Mood and quietness have little connection with this worship.

Our singing is not for the benefit of God, but to teach and admonish one another. Our prayers are for our needs and for the needs of others. Our giving is not to supply God's needs, but those of people. Our teaching is for the benefit of people. In the communion we renew our faith in the atonement and proclaim that atonement to others. These actions are done toward God only in the sense that Jesus expressed, "Truly, I say to you, as you did it to one of the least of these my brethren, you did it to me" (Matt. 25:40).

While exploring these ideas, it is good to recall that no assembly was referred to as a worship service by any inspired writer. They did not "go to worship," for their lives were a worship/service. The activities in their assemblies were for the benefit of those present. Read I Corinthians 14 carefully to see the repeated emphasis that all done in the assembly was to be for the upbuilding of the disciples. In verse 26, Paul instructs, "Let all things be done for edification." Those assemblies were not sessions of mystical communion with God, but a sharing with God's people. Attendance and participation is not to get our score card of righteousness checked, but to build up others and to be built up. Services and programs that do not accomplish either are meaningless, if not detrimental. The apportioning of our time and resources between the formal and informal worship/service in the committed life is left entirely to the judgment of the individual.

In limiting the concept of worship, I have quoted Colossians 3:17 countless times: "And whatever you do, in word or deed, do everything in the name of the Lord Jesus." I applied that to our exercises in the assembly, and there alone, as a demand for specific authority for each activity. However, the context is about the kind of life we should lead, with special directives to wives, husbands, children, and slaves. Then, in verse 23, he sums up, "Whatever your task, work heartily, as serving the Lord and not men." He calls for a whole-life honoring of our Lord as we wear His name.

I also coupled "whatever is not of faith is sin" with "faith comes by hearing, and hearing by the word of God" in a misapplication of scripture to limit the concept of worship. In the first passage, Paul is speaking of a person violating his conscience by going against his faith. In the second, Paul is urguing for the Gentile acceptance and universality of salvation proved by the fact that Christ sent His message and messengers to the Gentiles.

We have been warned many times by sincere teachers against additions to the five items of worship by use of the example of Nadab and Abihu, who were zapped for offering strange fire which the Lord had not commanded (Lev. 10:1-2; 16:12). However, persons were not punished for adding wine to the Passover meal (Lk. 22:14-18; Matt. 26:26-28), or for adding dancing before the Lord (2 Sam. 6:12-14; Psalms 149:3), or for adding the whole synagogue service. Nadab and Abihu had been given complete instructions which they defied. In the other examples, there was effort to honor God rather than to defy him.

How can worship be limited to five specifics, which are not so specific, when our bodies are to be presented as a living offering of worship?

In Lovington, New Mexico I had the unforgettable experience of being invited to speak to the Catholic youth group. I was allowed time to tell of my beliefs to be followed by a period for questions from the listeners. I was shown the utmost courtesy. In the question period, one of the sponsors asked, "If I should devise some personal way to let people know I was honoring Christ, so that each time they saw me, they would be reminded of my love for Him — some way — say, like wearing my hat sideways, would that be a sin?" How would you answer? I agreed that Christ could be honored that way.

I often wear a symbolic fish on my lapel to honor Christ. Some use appropriate plaques and bumper stickers. These can be worshipful expressions of praise and adoration. Some publish literature, write spiritual songs, make recordings of spiritual songs, do works of spiritually oriented art, or put beauty in a church building to honor Christ. These things stand as a continual expression of adoration, a living worship/service. Even after the worshipper has died, "he, being dead, yet speaketh."

One might keep a light in his window or tie a yellow ribbon around the old oak tree and let others know that these were symbols of his adoration to God. I have no reason to believe that God would be horrified at such a worshipful gesture. Again, our worship is not just in specific rituals or symbols, but in "whatever you do, in word or deed."

Whatever is designed to build up and strengthen our own faith or that of others can be acceptable worship/service — whether in the assembly or in daily life.

Let's give God the whole pie instead of a slice. In doing this, secular things become holy and God will be worshipped in the field and in the kitchen as was phophesied: "In that day shall there be upon the bells of the horses, 'Holy Unto Jehovah'; and the pots in Jehovah's house shall be like the bowls before the altar. Yea, every pot in Jerusalem and in Judah shall be holy unto Jehovah of hosts . . . " (Zech. 14:20-21).

Chapter 15

WORSHIP BY DEMAND

His children are torn between love and hate for their father. The father provides for his children well and, when they make additional requests, he listens and often gives what they ask for. He assures the children that he loves them. In response to this, they are grateful, obedient, and expressive of their love for him.

There is, however, something that tends to spoil this beautiful relationship. The father makes some unusual demands of the children. He requires that each week each child must say some complimentary things about him like "You are the greatest father in the world," "You really look handsome, Dad," or "You are very generous to us". Also, the father commands that on each Saturday night each child must give him a gift. He requires that the gift be boxed and wrapped in green paper and tied with a yellow ribbon.

If a child fails to meet all of these demands, he or she is scolded and warned never to be so indifferent to his demands again. If there is a repeated offense, the offending child is punished. One spring day his six year old girl was playing in the vacant lot next door where there were many wild flowers. She picked a bouquet of those flowers and, in her childish excitement, brought them to her father without thinking of the required box and wrapping. In extreme disgust the father threw the bouquet into the garbage and demanded an apology from the girl for being so presumptuous.

The art class of his nine year old son made posters which read, "Dad, I love you," to give to their fathers. Without thinking of his father's restrictions, he ran eagerly to his father and gave him the poster along with a big hug. The father shoved the child to the floor and tore the poster into bits while raving at the awe-stricken child about allowing other people to influence him to give unspecified gifts. An apology was demanded of the contrite child with the stern warning that, if he continued to let teachers and other kids lead him into such violations, he would be driven out of the home.

Once when the father's birthday fell on Tuesday, the twelve year old daughter made him a surprise birthday cake, wrapped it properly and presented it to him. He rejected the cake and rebuked her sternly, informing her that it was her own self-will rather than love that had caused her to do such a thing.

Now you can understand why the children are torn between love and hate for their father. They all secretly long for the day when they become sixteen so that they, like their sixteen year old brother, may run away from home. The father has a terribly selfish and egocentric personality problem and he is only using his children to build it up.

An Egocentric God

By now you surely recognize that I am not writing about family relationships. I have depicted the concept that many of our people have held about God and our worship and service as His children. Have we not portrayed our Father as having a colossal ego problem which would cause Him to demand our flattery to satisfy His vanity, to require our gifts to feed His pride, and to bind arbitrary whims to build up His sense of power? It is more of a picture of a child abuser than of a child lover. It puts praise, adoration, and devotion on a demand basis. This is one of the cruelest aspects of legalism. This concept was born of the legal ritualistic specifics of the Law of Moses, was developed by the medieval church, and was inherited by the reformers and restorers.

This philosophy has turned our assemblies into vertical services in our efforts to obey God's commands to worship Him. We have turned what should be edification into a system of rituals. Our successful achievement is in dotting each "i" and crossing each "t" so as to perform the ritual "well-pleasing in thy sight." But pleasing God through proper performance of rituals is not the purpose of our meetings together. Yet we have defined, refined, alienated, and divided over the ritualistic details in such practices as teaching and communion.

God has not instructed us to assemble for the purpose of

vertical communication. In the meetings, "Let all things be done for edification" (1 Cor. 14:26). Assemblies were never referred to as worship services in the New Testament writings. The disciples did not use our popular terminology such as "worship service", "meet to worship", or "begin our worship". Paul does speak of our whole-life offering as our worship/service. "I appeal to you therefore, brethren, by the mercies of God, to present your bodies as a living sacrifice, holy and acceptable to God, which is your spiritual worship" (Rom. 12:1). This refers not to assemblies and rituals but to whole life commitment with Jesus as Lord of our entire life.

What is the purpose of our meetings? Their purpose is not to fulfill arbitrary commands, to get our score card checked, or to merit approval by keeping holy details. Neither are they attended that we may receive imparted grace. In the sacramental system it is thought that when specified rituals are performed exactly as prescribed by law, grace is imparted into the heart of the worshipper. That erroneous concept still holds too many of us.

We do not attend meetings that we may carry on a vertical communion — a sort of mystical seance with God — like when persons participate in the Mass. Such persons enter the building quietly without noticing others, go to the end of the pew and genuflect to the presence of Christ in the Holy Eucharist, enter their pew, kneel, and begin their prayers. Then they leave in silence also. They neither understand nor seek to fulfill any purpose of communication with other worshippers.

In our gatherings we are to encourage one another, pray for one another, teach and admonish one another in song, teach one another, give to help one another, and proclaim the atonement to one another. Yet these activities are not more worship when done in the assembly than out of it. In these we fulfill the purpose of meetings which is to sustain the whole-life offering. In gatherings of disciples we may praise God, thank Him, and express reverential adoration. Such expressions are appropriate at any and all times whether in an assembly or not. But they are not the primary purpose of our fellowship gatherings.

God has no self-esteem problem that must be bolstered by

man's praise. God is concerned with saving man, not adding to His self-image. That which edifies man fulfills God's purpose. When God described Himself as a jealous God and pled that we should have no other gods before Him, He was not speaking out of a character defect in Himself. He was expressing His love for us and His desire for our full fellowship so He can save us. He wants no alienation of our affections lest we suffer the effects of sin eternally. God wants us to glorify Him — to hold Him in high opinion and to present Him in favorable aspect — not for His selfish satisfaction, but to cause others to come to Him. Thus Jesus urged, "Let your light so shine before men, that they may see your good works and give glory to your Father who is in heaven" (Matt. 5:16). It is for the good of man. His eternal purpose has been to restore man to fellowship with Himself. It is accomplished now in Christ. Edification helps us to sustain that fellowship.

Because of their very nature praise, adoration, and devotion cannot be demanded. "You praise me and give me gifts or I will consign you to eternal hell!" — is that the threat of our loving Father? Can threats bring forth praise? If God had demanded the last penny of the poor widow (Luke 21:1-4), we would see her appeasing a demanding God rather than offering an expression of devotion and love. If Mary had anointed Jesus with expensive nard to keep a law which demanded it, the beautiful example of undemanded and extravagant love and praise would have been lost (John 12:1-11). The sinful woman (Luke 7:36-50) might kiss Jesus' feet to keep a command, but tears do not come by command. Our praise, adoration, devotion, and worship is most appropriate when it is overflowing, spontaneous, and extravagant like that of those three women.

A father is pleased when his children thank him, compliment him, and give him gifts. But they demonstrate this love because of the father's favor, not to gain his favor. A rebellious child may give gifts to appease his father, but that becomes disgusting. We do not worship God to gain His favor but because He has shown His favor.

Many people are torn between love and hate for the Father because they have considered him as selfish and tyrannical, demanding praise and sacrifice. How different it is, however, when we can interpret our relation with him as an interaction of love!

Chapter 16

FREE EXPRESSION:

OUR RESPONSE TO GRACE

The obedience which glorifies God most beautifully is that which grows out of appreciation for what He has done for us. The loving response to His grace is a spontaneous overflowing of devotion. Undemanded, unrehearsed, and extravagant expressions gained Jesus' attention and received His commendation. The narratives concerning three women illustrate this and serve as examples to us. As we review these narratives we may see how our efforts to praise Him may be free expressions rising as an aromatic incense toward His throne.

1. On the sixth day before the Passover they made a supper for Jesus (John 12:1-11; Mark 14:3-9; Matthew 26:6-13). Mary took a pound of pure nard and anointed the head and feet of Jesus. The nard was worth three hundred denarii, about a year's wages for a laborer. Thus it was a very extravagant expression. As the fragance filled the house, it got the attention of everyone.

While Mary is the center of attention, let's interview her. "Mary, why did you do that?"

"I just felt like doing it," she answers with a glow in her countenance.

"Were you commanded to do it?"

"Certainly not!" she denies with a note of protest in her voice.

"Then don't you think that your action was presumptuous? If Jesus had wanted such a thing done, wouldn't He have told you to do it?"

"It is never presumptuous to express love to Him. Even that nard could not convey the real depth of my feeling for Him."

"But, Mary, wasn't that a big waste?"

"Sir, nothing is too big or wasted if it will let Him know how I love Him and if it will lift Him up in honor before others." Love is extravagant in its expressions.

"Don't you feel a bit guilty about it all, Mary?"

"No, I feel much happier. I felt badly until now because I had not communicated my love adequately."

"It was just for a big show!"

"Yes, I did it for show. I wanted to show Him and all of you my appreciation for Jesus."

"One more question, Mary. Wouldn't it have been more sensible to have used just a little of the perfume and to have saved the rest?"

"Love is not applied by an eye-dropper. Love is truly unselfish. It must be unmeasured."

The disciples joined Judas in scolding Mary for her action. How sad it is that we must demoralize those who do generous things simply because they do not meet our prejudicial notions. How chagrined the disciples must have been to hear Jesus intervene in Mary's defense, "Let her alone; why do you trouble her? She has done a beautiful thing to me. She has done what she could. Wherever the gospel is preached in the whole world, what she has done will be told in memory of her."

Mary's gift was beyond all practical value. Jesus recognized the value of aesthetic things. To lift our morale we spend much money on beauty in clothes, houses, cars, gifts, pictures, and flowers.

Sadi, a sheik who lived 700 years ago, understood this:

"If of thy mortal goods thou art bereft,
And from thy slender store two loaves alone to thee are left,
Sell one, and with the dole
Buy hyacinths to feed thy soul."

Often we hear the disciples join with Judas when someone wants to add a little beauty to our church buildings.

Mary's response was to grace, not law. The Rich Young Ruler is to be commended for his law-keeping, but he did not have the love to bring out the best in him. A marriage of the Marys and the Rich Young Rulers could change the church and the world.

2. "And he sat down opposite the treasury, and watched the multitude putting money into the treasury. Many rich people put in large sums. And a poor widow came, and put in two

copper coins, which make a penny" (Mark 12:41-44, Luke 21:1-4). Let's stop and interview this woman.

"Lady, why did you give your last penny?"

"I wanted to give special honor to God to show appreciation for all He has done for me," she replies.

"Were you commanded to give your last two coins — from a widow?"

"If I had such a demanding God as to require the last resources of a poor widow, frankly, I might not have had the desire to give them to Him at all." Love's offering is spontaneous.

"Lady, didn't you need that money?"

"Yes, and much more," she continues. "But I feel that this was more meaningful than to honor Him out of abundance." She did not check to see if she could afford to give. She was not smothered by caution.

"Come on now, do you expect me to believe this wasn't done to attract attention?"

"I did not know you were watching, or cared. I hoped that God would see my love for Him. It was to attract His attention!"

"But, lady, the law requires only a tithe. Why should you give more?"

"I might give to fulfill the law while showing no love. I wanted to express the deep feelings of love that I have for God."

And Jesus called His disciples to Him, and said to them, "Truly, I say to you, this poor widow has put in more than all those who are contributing to the treasury. For they all contributed out of their abundance; but she out of her poverty has put in everything she had, her whole living."

Mary's response was in emotional, extravagant beauty. The widow's response was selflessness. Love carries us out into the sea of boundless expression.

3. Jesus was invited to a meal at Simon's house (Luke 7:36-50). While He was eating, a sinful woman came in with an alabaster flask of ointment. "Standing behind Him at His feet, weeping, she began to wet his feet with her tears, and to anoint them with the ointment." Seeing this, Simon said to himself, "If this man were a prophet, he would have known who and

what sort of woman this is who is touching him, for she is a sinner."

We need not interview this woman. Jesus interviewed Simon and explained her motives in contrast to his. Jesus said, "Simon, I have something to say to you." He told of two debtors, one owing ten times as much as the other. When neither could pay, the creditor cancelled both debts. "Now which of them will love him more?" Jesus asked. Simon knew the right answer. "The one, I suppose, to whom he forgave more," he answered reluctantly.

"You have judged rightly," Jesus said. Then turning toward the woman He said to Simon, "Do you see this woman? I entered your house, you gave me no water for my feet, but she has wet my feet with her tears and wiped them with her hair. You gave me no kiss, but from the time I came in she has not ceased to kiss my feet. You did not anoint my head with oil, but she has anointed my feet with ointment. Therefore I tell you, her sins, which are many, are forgiven for she loved much; but he who is forgiven little, loves little."

We can imagine the protesting thoughts that might have jumped into Simon's mind. "Jesus, you did not tell me you wanted your feet washed. You did not command me to kiss you. The law does not require that I anoint your head. You know that I would have done these things . . . " That is the way I might have reasoned.

What was Simon's problem? Being a good Pharisee, he thought himself to have few, if any, sins. He needed little forgiveness, he thought. With such little cause for penitence, there would be no tears of sorrow nor of gratitude for mercy received. There would be little motivation for loving generosity. He would do his designated duties but he had nothing overflowing from his heart. No loving fragrance flowed from within him to fill the house. He only distracted from those whose emptied flasks filled the dismal room with heavenly perfume.

Did these three women illustrate the response to law or to grace? If these women had been seeking to keep requirements under threat of hell, Mary's perfume would have lost its fragrance, the widow's offering would have only been an effort to appease a demanding God, and the sinful woman would have had no tears with which to wet His feet. Neither action resulted from a guilt-prodding sermon. Their actions were as songs of praise divinely motivated. "Scared birds don't sing."

Our loving service is in response to grace. "If you love me you will keepmy commandments," but "We love because he first loved us." God's extravagant love is our motivation.

Chapter 17

LOWERING THE MORTALITY RATE

There is a great amount of concern about the high mortality rate of those born into the spiritual family. Many of us have tried to identify the cause of these losses in order to work on prevention and cure. It is good that we have this concern.

Prominent among the solutions offered is "Study the Bible more". It is generally concluded that a comprehensive course of indoctrination would take care of most of the problem. But the answer is not that simple.

Many of the dropouts have been knowledgeable of the Bible. There is a brilliant Bible major from one of our colleges who is widely known for his writings, but he has no part with us anymore. Once I went to hear a fifteen year old boy preach. I sat in amazement and admiration as this young man quoted scriptures as though he had the New Testament memorized. Several months later I made inquiry and learned that the young man had given up both his preaching and his discipleship. These are but two of the innumerable company who have known the Scriptures but have fallen away.

Are we suggesting that Bible knowledge is not important? By no means. But we are contending that the type of indoctrination is the big factor. There is little about knowledge of Biblical proof-texts concerning doctrinal controversies, quibbles, definitions and distinctions that gives strength to the character.

It is great to memorize the names of the books of the Bible, the tribes of Israel, the judges, kings, and apostles, but that is of little help to one who is discouraged and tempted.

Do you ever hear anyone say, "I think I never would have made it through my period of doubt and depression had I not known how to confute the Mormons and Jehovah's Witnesses at my door?"

"My son's ability to give scriptural answers against faith only, infant baptism, and sprinkling certainly kept him from falling away during those trying years while he attended the university," is another claim we are not likely to hear.

Being thoroughly indoctrinated concerning the one church, right rituals, right organization, qualifications of elders, and a cappella singing gives little stability to the woman whose marriage is in crisis.

When your sky caves in on you, you will gain little spiritual sustenance from your ability to refute the arguments of Calvinism, premillenialism, Pentecostalism, sacramentalism, cultism, and mysticism.

Such Comfort

One Sunday morning I taught a fifty-and-over class of about fifty persons. As an informal beginning, I invited the class to share favorite passages of Scripture which had given them faith, strength, courage, and comfort. There was a hestitation that became embarrassing. Then one man quoted the Great Commission, another Acts 2:38, another Matthew 7:21. After several such texts were recited, one lady finally came up with Romans 8:28. No wonder we fly apart in times of crisis!

I attended the funeral of a Christian woman in a small, but packed, building. The preacher spoke at length about the one church, the name, baptism, and call no man reverend. He made only one reference to the deceased and he called her by the wrong name then. Such comfort! I am glad to admit that this was an exceptional case. Yet one still detects this imbalance in church bulletins where more space is given to the junior high skating party than to the passing of a saint from the local church to heaven, and more space is used for indoctrination than for sharing sorrows.

Once there was a certain man who came to our services several times. He was a brother to a lady in the church. This lady came to me and explained that her brother was an alcoholic and had lost his family and his job because of it. She wished that I would have a sermon especially for him in reserve in case he should come again. I did. He came back. I was ready for him. I took the Bible and showed him what liquor would do for a person, how God felt about drunkards, and what their final address would be. He never came back. But I had cleansed my hands of his blood! Now I cringe to think how stupid I was. A drowning man had managed to surface in a frantic hope for help, and I yelled, "Get out of that water or you will drown!" I bound heavy burdens on the weakest man and did not extend my little finger to lift him out. I taught the truth, didn't I? But not the truth which could lift him out of slavery, humiliation, self-hatred, depression, and despair. I didn't have to tell him what liquor would do and where it would send him. He knew that better than I did. But I did not tell him of God's love and acceptance and what God could do for him. I did not offer him the loving embrace and shared strength of a hundred other disciples present. With his last strength, he struggled to the oasis in the burning desert and found it to be mirage. He perished of thirst beside what should have been the refreshing pool of the water of life.

The last pure joy many disciples experience is when they come up from the waters of baptism. They go on their way rejoicing until the next service. From there on it is a guilt trip. In each class and sermon each teacher makes it his studied aim to convince the disciple that he is not studying enough, not giving enough, not devoted enough, and not living cleanly enough. There is always the overshadowing cloud of fear of some misunderstood or neglected command. While these teachers may think that they are indoctrinating for strength, they may be succeeding in convincing the disciple that he can't make it. Then we wonder why he gives up.

Effective Bible learning must begin with faith building. Lives of Bible characters may be utilized to show the power of faith. God's love and promises must be made evident. God's grace should be the cheering message. Disciples must be convinced that their acceptance by God and other disciples is not based on merit. They should be made to realize the power of God, Christ, and the Holy Spirit in their lives. They should be taught the effectiveness of prayer and of Christian fellowship. Illustrations of the providence of God should give assurance and comfort. Realistic hope should develop patience and endurance. If Christian virtues are nurtured into the character, according to Peter, that person will neither fall nor be ineffective. You may continue to enlarge this list of resources that will initiate loving activity, strengthen the weak, lift the discouraged, cast out fears, carry one through dark trials, bring cheer to the despairing, and give assurance of a richly provided entrance into the eternal kingdom of our Lord and Savior Jesus Christ.

No person has been converted to a doctrinal stance entirely void of these strengthening elements. It is my conviction, however, that we have been overbalanced in that direction. A correction of this should help in lowering the mortality rate. It should help, but it will not eliminate the problem. Jesus' parable of the soils assures us that the mortality problem will be with us always.

Chapter 18

SALVATION IN DIFFERENT AGES

This lesson will be different from those I taught for many years concerning "the three dispensations." Those efforts covered some valid points but they did not reach the most accurate and complete conclusions. In this study I shall not pretend to reach the ultimate truth, but I hope you will explore with me and then give me your input.

When sin came and death came through sin, God designed to save man from both sin and death. In different ages God has saved man using different but related means and requirements. We offer this simple diagram for illustration as we proceed with this brief study.

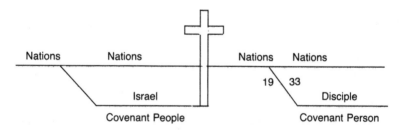

We begin with a line representing the races of humanity — the nations. Gentiles means nations, but since Gentiles is used in contrast to those who were of Israel, we will use the more general term nations in this discourse.

Along this line of the nations God has dealt with humanity in the entire course of history. In Old Testament history the nations had no offer of heaven or promise of personal salvation. There was no missionary, evangelical message with a plan of salvation or system of law. Intimations of immortality were dim.

Down through history God communicated with non-Israeli individuals such as Adam, Cain, Baalam, Beltshazzar, Nebuchadnezzar, the Magi, and Cornelius. Messages were sent to Nineveh, Egypt, Babylon, Assyria, Tyre, and Sidon.

Individuals of the nations worshipped God, such as Cain, Abel, Enoch, Noah, Abraham, Melchizedek, Jethro, and Job and on down through the Magi and Cornelius. The role of women and children in religion is vague along this line of the nations.

This line of God's dealing with the nations has continued from Adam until the present and it will end only when Jesus returns.

At one point God called Abraham from among the nations to create a separate nation. He made an agreement with Abraham based upon both earthy and spiritual promises and He sealed the agreement, or covenant, by circumcision, a mark to distinguish them from the nations (Gen. 19:9-14).

After Abraham's family multiplied and became Israel, God made an agreement with Israel (Deut. 4:11-14). The Law of Moses was given to guide the personal lives and worship of the covenant people. This law was not given to save them, and it could not, nor was it the covenant. It contained no plan of salvation, no missionary or evangelical message, nor any promise of heaven to the covenant people. Women and children had little part in it. This law was given only to the covenant people, not to the nations. Even though the law could bring sin and not salvation, ultimately Christ redeemed those who were under the law (Gal. 4:4-5). Thus their salvation was by grace instead of law. With the death of Jesus, that separated Israeli line ceased to exist. Since then there is no distinction as had been made by the covenant and the law. Now we are all in the original line of the nations of humanity.

This separation of the Israeli line from the line of the nations had not diminished God's interest in all men or reduced the accountability of the individual in the nations. God expected righteousness of them and he still requires righteousness of all men. But they had no revealed system of law or worship. How could they be counted as sinners since "sin is a transgression of the law" (1 John 3:4) and "where there is no law there is no transgression" (Rom. 4:15)?

They were obligated to the unwritten law. They had no code of law, but there are two ageless laws: Love God and love man. People who never heard of Moses or Christ have always been required to have these two laws written on their hearts. In Romans 2:14-27 Paul speaks of the Gentiles (nations) being a law unto themselves with the law written on the heart. Paul laid a charge against the nations for their lack of loving response in saying that, though they knew God through nature, they did not glorify him or give thanks, and then he enumerates their sins against one another (Rom. 1:20-32). They should have discerned that "God's kindness is meant to lead you to repentance" (Rom. 2:4). Even though, as it was with Nineveh, "The times of ignorance God overlooked, but now he commands all men everywhere to repent" (Acts 17:30), all individuals have not been commanded yet for an individual is not commanded who has not heard the command, hence, is still in "times of ignorance."

A man of the nations was not a sinner because of not keeping the Law of Moses, but he was lost because of his violation of the law which should have been written on his heart. Likewise, an unevangelized person today is not lost because he is not baptized or does not eat the Lord's Supper but because of his violation of love toward God and man. If he was not of the covenant people, he was not under the Law of Moses. If one is not in covenant relationship with God through Christ today, he is not under the directives given to the covenant people. He is a sinner because he has violated the unwritten law of love to God and man.

Aren't all people under the covenant of Christ today? Wasn't it ratified on the cross? A covenant relationship was made possible at the time of the atonement, but I was not living then in order to enter an agreement with God. I made my agreement with God in 1933, being separated to that line of God's covenant people. Then Jesus' directives given to regulate the covenant people became my guide. Previous to my sealing my covenant by baptism and his giving of the seal of the Spirit, I was not in the covenant of grace and was not judged or justified as a covenant person. I was not lost because I had failed to obey the gospel but because I was a sinner and could not save myself just as a person does not drown because he refuses the offered life preserver but because he is in the water and cannot swim out.

Those who "obey not the gospel" (2 Thes. 1:7-9) are not lost because of violation of Jesus' teachings but because they are sinners who reject the only means of salvation. The gospel is the good news. It is God's invitation to enter a covenant relationship through Christ. One is not condemned by it but he is saved by it. He who disbelieves the gospel will be damned (Mark 16:16) because he is already a sinner and he rejects the offered salvation. Neither the gospel nor the commands, exhortations, warnings, and teachings given to regulate the life of the disciple were the cause of my being a sinner in the first place. The nations and I were "strangers to the covenants of promise, having no hope and without God" (Eph. 2:12) but they and I became "members of the same body, and partakers of the promise in Christ Jesus through the gospel" (Eph. 3:6). That is equally true of all those who have become disciples.

Could a Gentile be saved before Christ came? No. Neither could a Jewish law keeper. However, it was of the nations that Paul wrote, "For he will render to every man according to his works: to those who by patience and well-doing seek for glory and honor and immortality, he will give eternal life . . . but glory and honor and peace for every one who does good, the Jew first and also the Greek. For God shows no partiality" (Rom. 2:6,7,10,11). "So, if a man who is uncircumcised keeps the precepts of the law, will not his uncircumcision be regarded as circumcision?" (Rom. 2:26). Although it is not stated positively in Romans 2 that Gentiles will be saved, it is strongly implied by Paul. How could they be saved since they had lived without promise? They could be saved by the same grace that saved the Jew who had no promise of salvation under the law. If God sent his son "to redeem those who were under the law" who kept it imperfectly, could we not expect the same grace toward those who had the law written on the heart but kept it imperfectly? And if that grace prevailed in the past, may we not expect it to prevail in the future? That is the only hope that any of us has.

No person will be saved apart from the atonement of Jesus Christ, yet the Jew who kept the law imperfectly and the Gentile who kept the law written on the heart imperfectly reaped the benefit of the atonement without having had personal knowledge or acceptance of Jesus or a personal relationship with him. The mercy of God could not have demanded that which was impossible of them. There is comfort in believing that God still does not demand the impossible.

Chapter 19

THE IDENTITY OF THE CHURCH

Many times I have pulled out my yellowed outlines and sought to convince my audience of the identity of the Church of Christ with the one true church. In time I have come to realize that many of the marks of identity that I stressed were secondary characteristics and not of primary significance.

Most of the treatments of the identity of the church that I have heard or read dealt with an organizational concept of the church. An organization can be traced historically and may identify historically. The church, however, is a "here and now" relationship of people with God. It is a present, living organism. It has roots in history but does not gain its life or identity from those roots.

There were predictions of falling away. "Now the Spirit expressly says that in later times some will depart from the faith . . . " (1 Tim. 4:1). Concerning the coming of the day of the Lord, Paul assured, "for that day will not come, unless the rebellion comes first" (2 Thes. 2:1-4). There was to be a rebellion or falling away of some. But how extensive was that to be? Would it be some or all individuals, or some churches, or a universal obliteration of the church?

If the concept of the restoration of the church is built upon the premise that the church was totally fallen away from the faith, then some scripture teachings would need more explanation. Daniel predicted that "the God of heaven shall set up a kingdom which shall never be destroyed . . . and it shall stand forever" (Dan. 2:44). The writer of Hebrews exhorts, "Let us be grateful for receiving a kingdom that cannot be shaken" (Heb. 12:28). How could the kingdom be declared to be non-existent through most of the centuries since its founding, like from Constantine in the fourth century until Campbell in the nineteenth century, in view of these passages? Alexander Campbell considered himself a reformer, not a restorer of the church. He believed that "the gates of hell shall not prevail against it" (Matt. 16 :18). He sought to restore the unity which had been spoiled among disciples.

The church has been in need of constant reform since its earliest days. The epistles were written to congregations needing redirection. Because the church is people, there will always be error and misdirection which will need to be corrected.

As the centuries passed, many doctrinal and practical changes came to be accepted. Because of the development of bishop rule, these erroneous teachings and practices could be bound on the church universally. So it happened. The question now is: Did deviations make it no longer the church? Was its identity destroyed? If so, when? When did the church lose its essence, or essential nature?

To illustrate this matter, as Leroy Garrett once proposed, let us explore what is the essential nature of a man. Here is a man. We amputate a leg. Is he still a man? We add glasses. Is he still a man? We pull his teeth out and substitute man-made dentures. Has that changed his essential nature? He changes his name. Is he still a man — the same man? He has cancer, is addled by a fever. Has he ceased to be a man? Many other physical, mental, and social changes might affect his quality as a man but they would not destroy the essential nature of a man.

Now, let's think of the essential nature of a church. It has only one elder. Is it still a church? It binds the holy kiss. Is it a church now? It changes its name. Has it ceased to be a church? It is filled with jealousy and strife. Has that destroyed its identity? It burns votive candles. Has that changed its essential nature? It accepts tongue speaking and belief in miraculous healing. Is it still a church? Many other deviations of belief and practice might change its quality as a church but they would not destroy the essential nature of a church.

These changes in the man and the church are not changes in the essence of either, but they are changes in secondary characteristics. Secondary characteristics are always in need of purification and reform; however, deviations do not always destroy the identity. While it is our role to reform, only the Lord is able to judge and remove the candlestick.

The Essence

What is the essence of the church? Stripping off all secondary characteristics, what will we discover to be the real church? What is essential? The essential nature of the church is that it is those in Christ. Being baptized into Christ, His body, His church, persons are saved, being added by the Lord Himself (Acts 2:38,47; Rom. 6:3-4; 1 Cor. 12:13; Col. 1:18). The church is those who have been redeemed. They are not perfected in belief or practice but, serving sincerely, they are continually cleansed (1 John 1:7-10) and are made to stand (Rom. 14:4). According to Romans 14, we are not to judge or disdain those in Christ who differ in belief and practice. There is need of constant reform. There are proper causes for rejection, withdrawal, and delivering to Satan which we discussed in the previous chapter titled "Our Creed". These drastic actions are to be taken only against those who renounce the faith, abandon moral purity, or become divisive. These actions are not to be taken against ignorant, misguided, stumbling disciples who are sincerely trying to do the will of their God who happen to be in error on convictions different from yours or mine.

Some of my earliest remembrances while growing up on a cotton farm near Rochester in West Texas were of attending revival meetings. The people of that small community built a "tabernacle", as we called it. It was like a house without walls, a superstructure somewhat like a tent without the side flaps. Each church had its turn to use it for gospel meetings.

A Union Meeting

Three of the churches joined forces to have a "union meeting". They chose a preacher who agreed not to preach any of their distinctive denominational messages. Even though I was only a young child, I can recall how the preacher would bring laughter, then tears, and, in his concluding appeal, fright. Many would respond and were saved supposedly. After the concluding service the chairman said something to this effect: "We have had a great number saved. Now it is time for you who were saved to join the church of your choice. Brothers A, B, and C, preachers of the cooperating churches, will stand in these different locations at the front. You may present yourself to one of these men and he will tell you how to join his church."

Now, let us suppose we have a union meeting similar to that one but different in some details. Three churches cooperate in it. They get a preacher who promises to preach no doctrine except from the Bible. He will just preach the gospel like Peter did on Pentecost. The meeting is a great success. Eighty persons believe, repent, confess faith in Christ, and are baptized for the remission of their sins. Everyone is rejoicing.

Then the final service is completed and the chairman arises and says, "Many have been saved. Now it is time for you to join the church of your choice. The preachers for churches A, B, and C will stand here before you. All who wish to join A church come with Brother A." Twenty arise and stand with him. Brother B is introduced and twenty stand with him. Brother C rejoices inwardly because he thinks he is to get the remaining forty. But when he is introduced, only twenty stand with him.

At this point there is an air of perplexity about the remaining twenty. The chairman inquires of them, "Aren't you going to join a church?"

"No," they respond, "we are in the church already."

"How can that be?" the chairman asks.

"So far our preacher has preached the gospel like Peter did on Pentecost. When people were baptized for the remission of sins then, they were saved, being baptized into Christ and his one body which is the one church. We have done only what they did and we trust that we are in the same church that they were added to. Now you are going beyond the scriptures in urging us to join sectarian divisions. All eighty of us are in the one church, being added by the Lord himself. To join different groups now and to wear names to distinguish us from one another is to become divided, sectarian, and denominational."

"Well, you are starting a new church, are you?" the chairman asks, not quite able to grasp the explanation.

"No, we are just remaining in the one the Lord added us to. We will not exclude the other saved persons or wear a distinguishing name."

"What, then, are you going to do?"

"We will continue to teach, learn, and grow, meeting together in fellowship and in worship. We will lead clean lives and try to demonstrate the love of Jesus' disciples. We will seek to do all the will of God. And we invite the other sixty saved persons and all other saved persons to be with us in this fellowship in Christ."

That illustrates the essence of the church, free from sectarian distinctiveness. It has a "here and now" identity. It is not a matter of tracing the church back through the Restoration Movement and certainly it cannot be, and need not be, traced back to Pentecost as an organized body. Wherever there were saved people in any century, there was the church. The church is the saved, here and now, and at any time and place in history.

To divide the saved into groups as we have illustrated is to create sects. The Restoration Movement has begun as an effort to bring the saved in all those sects back into unity.

When a person is in Christ, he should be free from sectarian Christianity.

"THE SEED IS THE WORD"
Christ's church is sparkling new,
Yet we're nineteen centuries old,
Like wheat which this year grew,
And has for years untold

Though time may kill each crop,
Another fills our need,
Not by perpetual plant,
But by life-giving seed.

-Cecil Hook

Chapter 20

THIS LESSON SCARES ME!

If a lesson does not raise eyebrows, it is likely to droop eyelids. Many of mine have left me and others with the drooping eyes. This lesson, however, raises my eyebrows. In fact, it scares me. I think that it will bring some shock to you also if I can hold your attention through some necessary contextual background. So please hang on.

Paul dealt with several problems among the Corinthian saints in his first letter to them. The thematic issue of the letter is the disintegration of the unity of the one body.

Those who "were called into the fellowship of his Son" were becoming factional (1:9-17). Instead of speaking/saying the same thing in saying "I am of Christ," they were speaking diversely in identifying themselves with factional leaders. Paul, Apollos, and Cephas were not the party leaders, though Paul used the names of innocent men in a literary device to give the guilty ones opportunity to correct their conduct with the least loss of face (4:6f). Later, although Paul never names those impenitent leaders, he does speak of them as "false apostles, deceitful workers" in his second Corinthian epistle (11:13f).

In the third chapter, Paul deals with the disciples' carnality as was in evidence because of their jealousy, strife, and factionalism (3:1-3). They, as a body, were God's temple and anyone who would destroy the unity of that body would be destroying the dwelling place of the Holy Spirit (3:16f). That's not referring to cigarette smoking. That's talking about polarizing God's people! This is already a bit scary, isn't it?

Paul would have none to be "inflated with pride as you patronize one and flout the other" (4:6 NEB).

After dealing with other problems and misunderstandings, Paul returns to his theme of unity (10:16-22). Since the communion is the participation in the body and the blood of Christ, it becomes a symbol of the unity of the communicants. "We are one bread/loaf." One can visualize Paul holding the unbroken bread before the assembly and saying with deep feeling, "We are one loaf."

Here is where factionalism showed itself in all its ugliness. One group would not wait for the others. The parties disdained each other in the love feast and communion. Their participation was for the worse, not for the better (11:17-22). Paul shamed them, " . . . there must be factions among you in order that those who are genuine among you may be recognized." The genuine disciples would be conspicuous by their lack of party alignment. Because their eating together had become a demonstration of factional loyalty, it could not really be called the Lord's Supper; it became their own sectarian supper.

The remainder of Chapter 11 is familiar to all, but let's look at some of the expressions used. Here are the one loaf and one cup depicting the one body and its life-blood. Whoever eats or drinks it in an unworthy manner is guilty of profaning the body and blood. The "unworthy manner" or "unworthily" describes the action rather than the person. In action, they were factional. What should have been participation by all was limited by each group to those approved within the group. They were eating and drinking without "discerning the body" — without discerning the oneness, the unity of the body. Without respecting the unity of the body, they were eating and drinking condemnation to themselves.

This interpretation of the meaning of "unworthily" is not the traditional one, but is it not in harmony with the wider context which includes Chapters 12, 13, and 14?

These thoughts send a shudder through my soul as I recall the many distinctions, factions, and divisions that have plagued our people. It is true that, even though there were factions in congregations, we have usually communed together as long as we were in the same building. But after separating in different localities, what communion that has been maintained has been no more than a patronizing tolerance toward those on the right and an utter disdain for those on the left.

For many years I taught with an innocent smugness that we

do not believe in "closed communion." Anyone who attends may judge himself and decide on his participation. So far, so good — as long as it is our building, our service, our Lord's Supper. But will I go to their building, their service, their Lord's Table? Now I begin to make all kinds of rationalizations as to why I should not do so. I justify my factionalism. I refuse to discern the oneness of the body. By this, my participation/communion/fellowship in my own setting becomes an expression and reinforcement of factional loyalty. When it is not my loyal group, I suddenly come to believe in closed communion. That scares me! How can we be in communion/fellowship with one who is not of the Church of Christ when he comes to our service and then deny that fellowship at all other times? If we accept him on his self-examination at the Lord's Table, why can't we accept him on that basis at all times?

When I become the judge of another brother to exclude him, I disregard Paul's warning, "Let a man examine himself, and so eat of the bread and drink of the cup." Those disciples in Corinth misunderstood and disagreed on some important doctrinal matters, but Paul made that no basis to justify refusal of communion with each other and for dividing the one body. Do we have issues of greater vitality than circumcision, eating of meats, observance of days, and those differences in the Corinthian church? Paul would not let the saints judge each other on such matters. Read Romans 14 again.

We try to sweep this troublesome problem under the rug by meeting in separate assemblies so that we can be with our approved group without admitting that the body is divided, but we are still sectarian exclusivists in mind and practice.

The turning point in the thinking of Thomas and Alexander Campbell was over the problem of their Presbyterian factions refusing to commune with other Presbyterians. Thomas reached his decision in America while Alexander reached his independently in Scotland. So they began their efforts to restore the unity of the disciples in the different factions. It is ironic that the movement that started in rejection of closed communion should become entrapped by it again.

Yes, this scares me! And it depresses me deeply because I

have shared the guilt of my people.

As I commune now, however, I not only think of the atonement of Christ, but also of my communing/sharing/fellowship with Christ and all persons on earth who have received His grace. I am free from judging them. We are one body — one bread/loaf — which can allow for no factional loyalties.

Chapter 21

SERVANTS THAT BECAME RULERS

There are three servants that have become our masters, yea, four came to serve God's people and stayed to rule. These servants that betrayed us are (1) the Sunday School, (2) the paid ministry, (3) the church building, and (4) the budget.

Good and expedient devices and methods can be used in accomplishing our spiritual objectives. These devices and methods, however, should serve our needs rather than taking over individual responsibility, limiting individual initiative, or becoming a yoke upon our necks. These four servants have violated the trust we placed in them.

I. THE SUNDAY SCHOOL. I recall as a child when Bible classes came to our area. Many sincere disciples thought it sinful to divide the assembly in order to teach. Most congregations added classes anyway, and the system developed to the extent that many sincere disciples consider it a sin not to attend the classes. I suppose a fellow has lived too long when he lives from the time that it is wrong to attend classes to the time that it is wrong not to attend them.

Bible classes were organized to supplement home and individual teaching. They were an aid to the parent. But gradually, through our undiscerning promotion of them, they took over the responsibility of the home. Most Christian homes, I fear, have no regular teaching. If parents shift the responsibility to the church, the class is no longer a servant — the supplement; it becomes the ruler in the child's spiritual education. And when the church program seems ineffective, the parent can complain, "The church is not doing enough for my child," and can change to another congregation that has a greater youth program.

God's youth program is the family, his school is the home, and his teachers are the parents. If parents take ten minutes a day in reading, teaching, praying, and interacting spiritually with their children, they will accomplish much more than perfect attendance in the church program can do.

Parental teaching makes spirituality a part of real life. Otherwise, we impress on our children that religion is in another realm — in a church building, only with church people, in a holy King James Version sort of language, needing professionals, who often employ an unnatural preacher tone. But the home is where the daily life is, and parental interaction makes it practical. It makes religion daily life centered rather than weekly/semi-weekly and church centered. And parents can better adapt the training to the needs of the individual child.

It would be hard to re-establish the practice of this parental responsibility, but it wasn't easy to build the Bible class system to take over the responsibility. If we will spend only a fraction of the effort, time, emphasis, and money to re-establish parental teaching as we have done to enthrone and maintain the class system, it will be accomplished. Then classes can become servants again.

2. PAID MINISTRY. If we are not to muzzle the ox — the elder who labors in preaching and teaching — but consider that "The laborer deserves his wages" (1 Tim. 5:17f), then the validity of a paid ministry is established. Such occupational service enlarges and supplements the labors of others. Corporately, the disciples may accomplish what they cannot do individually. But the individual responsibility comes first. When the individual responsibility is surrendered to the church program, then the servant has become the master.

In 1 Corinthians 9, Paul affirms the right of supported evangelists, but the great apostle and evangelist showed us a preferred way by being a tentmaking evangelist.

Our Movement began and thrived with few church-supported ministers. Elders and other capable persons taught and edified the congregations. Support was given to the evangelists more commonly. Gradually, the emphasis was shifted and support for evangelism was supplanted by support for the ministry. Many of us still call ourselves evangelists/preachers, but our primary function is to minister to the saved. Ministry has gained priority, and only after the ministry is satisfied do we generally consider supporting evangelism.

The minister has become essential. No congregation is thought to have a chance of success without a paid professional. A small congregation will scream nation-wide for help to support a minister to save it from doom and to promise it prosperity. A formal pulpit message is considered a necessity twice each Sunday. There are countless non-professional ministers who are qualified and willing to serve the pulpits of churches throughout our nation, but they are not used because they are not professionals. The preaching talents of men are bid for in salary like star athletes while the mission fields go begging.

The teacher's role is not quite as important today as it was in New Testament times. The message was in Spirit-directed men then. The extant scriptures had to be read and taught to the illiterate public. Now most everyone has a Bible and can read it for himself, and he has literature, tapes, films, video, radio, and television to help him. Our pulpit method has become institutionalized.

We think to improve the work of the congregation by supporting men for all the ministries — youth, education, jail, singles, aged, personal evangelism, counselling, secretarial work, janitorial work, and so forth. These are fine as long as they supplement and aid the efforts of the members of the body. But the servant easily becomes the master as the individuals relinquish their work to those paid to do it. Services rendered by hired personnel cannot convey personal love and discipleship like those rendered through personal initiative. The members hire these professionals to do their work and, when the program does not thrive, the professional is replaced by one who offers greater promise, even if a higher salary is needed to get him. The various gifts in the body are smothered and the function as a body becomes sluggish.

I realize fully that I am undermining my own life-long work by what I am writing. The professional ministry has become ruler in my lifetime. I have helped to develop the problem and I am now willing to help to solve it.

Any claims that the church cannot thrive without a paid ministry were disproved in our Movement in the last century, and are disproved today by the Mormons who, without paid personnel, are growing faster and larger than we are.

3. THE CHURCH BUILDING. There is no mention of church-owned property in the New Testament writings and secular writers mention church buildings early in the third century. Some place to meet is necessary, whether the church owns or rents the building or meets in private quarters. The building serves a need, but this servant has raised from its obscure beginning to become a tyrant, ruling many congregations with a strangle hold.

Many of us can remember when our buildings were cracker boxes, causing us to develop an inferiority complex about our buildings. So it is more a matter of pride than wisdom that moved us to put our money into real estate. We have come to equate success with the size of our physical plant even though it is never filled and is used only four out of each 168 hours each week — or less!

Too, we have been few in number in small congregations. So we developed a pride in numbers also. As our congregations have grown in size, we have felt it imperative to have all the members meet at the same time. This has multiplied the expense of our structures several times. A church plant that cares for 300 persons can care for a thousand or fifteen hundred by having multiple assemblies. The savings on auditorium, classrooms, parking, utilities, and upkeep can release many thousands of dollars for evangelism and benevolence in most congregations. The building is king, living sumptuously off the financial resources while missions and the needy beg for the crumbs that fall from the table. We hear of million dollar collections for buildings. Would it not be nice to hear churches boast of million dollar collections for evangelism and missions? But we love our king!

4. THE BUDGET. The idea of a church budget is foreign to the scriptures. Special collections were taken for the poor, and some help was sent to Paul to help in his evangelistic activities. There is no indication that these were perpetuated in a regular budgeted program. These examples indicate that we may pool our resources in a congregation to do a corporate work too large for the individual. A common treasury can aid and supplement

the work of individuals. But this servant has grown to be a demanding ruler.

Primary responsibility for caring for the hungry, sick, aged, widow, orphan, and destitute is placed on the individual. In serving these we serve Christ. That is the character of pure religion. But now the church has taken these ministries and put them in a budgeted program — usually about 2% of the budget — and demands our money to expedite them. So now, if a person who is hungry, sick, or needs rent or utilities paid approaches a member for help, the member explains, "What you would have gained from me is given to God! (Matt. 15:1-9). I can't help you. I have given my money to the church. Go to the church where perhaps you can be included in the impersonal program budgeted by the church."

We have even heard disciples warned against "eldering their own money," insisting that they should do their work through the church "so Christ will get the glory!" So we give to the church rather than to persons. But churches don't have religion; only individuals have religion. The church has wrested these personal responsibilities from its members, robbing them of the joy of service and the demonstration of concern which is so convincing to the lost.

Someone may think that the church would be left to wither away and die if we dethroned these four rulers. But look at the New Testament writings again. There you will discover that the church did not depend upon Bible classes, paid ministry, church buildings, or budgets; yet it took the Roman Empire without these rulers! The Restoration Movement became the fourth largest religious body in America in the nineteenth century with little aid from these four methods and devices. We may think that it couldn't happen, but it did.

In our effort to get back to basics, it would be wise for us to reconsider the place of those things, especially in view of the fact that we are losing ground since becoming enslaved to those servants. We cannot expect the masters to free us, nor can we abandon commitments already made or the buildings already in use. Change of course will be gradual. Let us start by giving new stress to individual responsibilities.

Chapter 22

FLEXIBILITY IN ORGANIZATION

Recently, an elder told me that, if a church had an unscriptural elder in it, the entire congregation would be in sin — even the teenagers! Like so many others, he believes that the church is an organization and that we relate to God through a certain pattern of organization. Our traditional pattern of independent congregations, each with elders and deacons, is often viewed as a life-or-death matter. Any flexibility would be unthinkable. But where in the New Testament is such emphasis placed upon organization? Our saving relationship is with Christ rather than an authority structure men. Where is an exclusive pattern set forth and enjoined? God could have outlined one plainly, but he did not choose to do so. Why should we seek to make access to Christ through specified organization?

This traditional interpretation says that all churches with qualified men must appoint them as elders with open-ended (lifetime) tenure by nomination and lack of "scriptural objection written out and signed." The nominations are often made by the existing elders. When appointed, these elders are given authority in many churches to make binding decisions which the congregation must support under threat of hell. All of this is much more traditional than scriptural, however.

Those who are saved in Christ are not an organization, but they may organize the cooperative work of individuals. As they band themselves together for mutual edification and work, no inflexible structural pattern is necessary to identify them as the Lord's disciples. In its simple form a church may be only a mother and her children with no organized program of work or assemblies outside the home. A group of women may compose a congregation like Lydia and her household did in the beginning in Philippi. In Romans 16, Paul sends greetings to what we may call house churches, and there is no indication in the epistle of any larger assembly or organization comprising the church in Rome.

Jerusalem presents a more complex picture of the church, though it is not in conflict with the Roman picture. Early in Acts, there were 5,000 men (4:4), which number "multiplied greatly" (6:7). Some writers suggest the possibility of 100,000 disciples in the Jerusalem church. They could hardly have met in one assembly. In fact, we know that they met from house to house (Acts 2:46; 5:42; 8:3). Yet we never read about churches (plural) in Jerusalem; it is always the church. These house groups operated within the framework of the Jerusalem church. They could have their house meetings for their general activities and still be involved in the city-wide fellowship. A house church could appoint an elder or elders, and any and all elders in these groups would be included in the mention of the elders of the church in Jerusalem. All of these small (and larger) groups would be cooperating through their elders with all others in the city. Since no mention is made of separate groups of elders, it seems emphatic that there was only one body of elders in Jerusalem while, at the same time, it is emphatic that there were various places of meeting. There were centralized gatherings for preaching and teaching in the temple (Acts 2:46; 5:20,25,42), but it would be unrealistic to suppose that thirty, sixty, or ninety thousand disciples met there on a regular basis. Although we read of the "whole church" being assembled in the Jerusalem conference (Acts 15:22), we can hardly demand that this included all the many thousands of disciples in one assembly. It must mean that the whole church was there representatively.

A congregation may have no elders, or only one elder. Another might appoint deacons to serve it while having no elders, even as they did in Jerusalem in earlier times. One church might be overseen by an evangelist. Then, there may be churches following our traditional pattern with a highly organized program. One church may work independently while others may choose to share in certain efforts. None of the alternatives suggested here are set forth as an exclusive pattern, but they are an indication of great flexibility and adaptability of groups of disciples.

To those who believe there is a strict pattern, some of the above may sound very shocking. But hold on; the quake is not over! There is no command or instruction in the New Testament for a church to appoint elders, nor is there an example of a church appointing elders. The qualifications of elders were not written to congregations or to existing elders. "Elders in every city" (Titus 1:5) does not necessarily mean a plurality in every congregation for there might be numerous churches or house groups in the city. "Elders (plural) in every city" is not equivalent to "elders in each city." In this state, mayors are elected in every city, but no one understands that to mean that mayors (plural) are elected in each city. "Husbands, love your wives" (Eph. 5:25) does not obligate a man to love a plurality of wives, nor for a wife to have a plurality of husbands. Although Paul and Barnabas ordained elders in every church (Acts 14:23), they did not command that this be a universal practice. There were elders in the Jerusalem church, but that did not mean that there were elders in each house church which composed it. If that is a binding example, then we can have no church without elders, for they appointed them in "every" church. No mention is made of tenure. Elders were not given authority to legislate, binding decisions. No one stands between a man and his God; we are all equals before him. Although some versions use the word "rule" relating to their work, that word carries the meaning of leadership rather than authority.

There is instruction for an evangelist to appoint elders (Titus 1:5) and there is example of evangelists appointing them (Acts 14:23). The qualifications of elders were sent to the evangelists, Timothy and Titus, rather than to elders or churches.

Timothy was at Ephesus when Paul wrote to him. There were elders in Ephesus before that time. Why did Paul not send the description of elders to the existing elders in Ephesus instead of sending it to Timothy? Why not include the description in the Ephesian letter instead of Timothy's letter? When Paul spoke to the Ephesian elders at Miletus previous to his writing to the Ephesians and Timothy, he warned that some of the elders would become destructive (Acts 20:24-30). Their correction was not left to the Ephesian church or the other elders, but the evangelist was to hear the charges and give public rebuke against those elders who persisted in sin. The evangelist was to exercise that authority, being cautious about whom he would appoint, laying hands on no one hastily. This was a task of such magnitude as to give the young evangelist nervous indigestion or ulcers. So he would need a little wine to settle his nerves. Amen! (1 Tim. 5:17-23).

Elders are not necessary. They are expedients. A church might carry on its activities for many years in a democratic way. Its decisions are not law, but the group only asks for unity of spirit and loyalty. Later, it may appoint men to oversee the group, and these elders may decide to continue the same program of activity. The decision of the elders is no more binding than was that of the general meeting. They can only continue to call for unity and loyalty.

Then why have elders? (1) As a group grows in number, its oversight becomes more cumbersome. A smaller group of men can expedite its activities better. (2) The group can choose men who have greater talent, leadership, understanding, and spirituality for greater efficiency. These are reasons of judgment and expediency.

Servants - Deacons - Ministers

Deacons are necessary. Anyone who fills an appointed capacity is a servant of that church. We would do well to forget that synthetic, prejudicial word "deacon", which is the anglicized Greek word for servant or minister. A deacon is a servant, and to serve is to minister. A servant/deacon/minister (SDM) is one who serves. A SDM of the church is one who is appointed to serve by the church rather than an office or standing committee. A man appointed to keep the treasury, lead singing, serve Lord's Table, or mow the lawn is a SDM. A woman who teaches a class, keeps the nursery, or publishes the bulletin is a SDM.

I have heard and read of various efforts to give a job description for deacons. They are always strained and vain searches for clues to uphold a traditional concept. The only job description is in the words servant or minister. Some servants (traditional deacons) do not serve while others who serve are not servants (traditional deacons). Much of our confusion stems from our legalistic interpretation of the qualifications of a SDM (1 Tim. 3:8-13). Paul is saying that only upright persons should represent the congregation in any capacity of service. He or she has a stamp of approval when appointed for public activity, so "Do not be hasty in laying on of hands" (1 Tim. 5:22) lest we be partakers of the sins of unworthy persons who have been approved by their appointment.

An absurdity of our interpretation is evident when we choose a pulpit SDM or song leader whom we will not call a servant (traditional deacon) because he has no children. Others, because they have children are appointed as servants (traditional deacons) in name who often are assigned no area of service; yet these fill an office and are listed on the stationery letterhead!

A person is a SDM of the church only in the area assigned to him or her. When that work is completed, the appointment is fulfilled and he or she is no longer a SDM.

Women have been included by Paul as those who qualify "likewise" or "in like manner" for congregational service (1 Tim. 3:11). Application of this passage to deacons' wives is an evasion born of legalistic interpretation. Why would Paul give requisites for a SDM's wife and be silent about an elder's wife?

With both men and women, it boils down to this: no job assigned — no SDM; keeping an assignment — a SDM. All of us serve the Lord, but all do not have congregational assignment; hence, all are not servants of the church.

A church with no elders can give assignments even as the church in Jerusalem chose servants for a specific work (Acts 6:1-6). A church must have servants, if it carries on any organized activity.

It is hoped that the preceding thoughts will cause you to see that our traditional refinements are not necessarily the last word or the model for all others. God has allowed some flexibility even though you don't hear much about it from our pulpits. It is tedious to teach anything unsettling about the elders and deacons within the congregation. When you are supported by the system, you must support the system. No marvel that Timothy needed a little wine.

Methods of carrying on church business and of selecting elders are not specified in the scriptures. Much of it seemed to be the responsibility of the evangelist, but the "located preacher" of today does not necessarily correspond with the evangelist of the New Testament. The evangelist brought the gospel to them; hence, he was the mainstay in the formation of the congregation. This is the role that Paul, Barnabas, Timothy, and Titus filled which qualified them to appoint elders. The Corinthian disciples were to recognize and be subject to the household of Stephanas because of their work and stability in developing the church there (1 Cor. 16:15-18). Read the epistles to Timothy and Titus to see that evangelists exercised the authority of leadership. They would have already proved their love, their understanding of the group, and their ability to lead. So they would lead in the organizing of congregational activity. They would consult with and gain approval of the congregation as to who would qualify for appointment. Congregational independence and autonomy seem evident in the Scriptures, so we my conclude that any method which preserves those qualities is permissible today. Since this is left to judgment in the various congregations, we must allow for flexibility, for all will not have the same judgment.

Chapter 23

AUTONOMOUS OR EPISCOPAL

While we talk much about our congregations being autonomous, in reality many are episcopalian in government.

Autonomy is self-government. Elder/bishop rule is episcopal/presbyterian rule. For a congregation to be autonomous, the members must approve those who are appointed to capacities of leadership and they must continue to exercise the right of approving or recalling those who are serving. Once either of these rights is forfeited, autonomy has faded and episcopacy has set in.

We tend to confuse independence with autonomy. A group may be independent of all others and not be autonomous, even as a nation may be independent, but because it is ruled by a non-elected king or dictator, it is not autonomous. The earthly operation of the church is democratic even though in its spiritual form it is a kingdom with Christ as King.

If the will of the majority is not served, then self-government is lost to minority rule. If elders assume power to bind decisions on a church, that is episcopal rule and lordship. If they exercise authority contrary to the will of the majority, they are lording it over the flock. The elder who serves unwanted by a large segment of the congregation is lording.

If elders are to be put in the role of decision makers for the group, their decisions must forever remain in the realm of judgment. A work program or schedule of services set forth by the elders is no more authoritative and binding than one set forth by a business meeting in a church that has no elders. To exercise the power to bind these judgmental decisions would rob a congregation of its sacred right of self-government. If elders, whether in a house church with one elder or a congregation with several, serve as pastors/shepherds to the spiritual need of the flock instead of being rulers/decision makers/business managers, they will be serving their intended purpose. Thus, no longer being authority figures, they will be removed from the power structure and struggles that involve them in so much controversy.

Elders are chosen to oversee the congregation, but a church cannot empower men to legislate for it. A minority cannot rightly choose men to oversee the whole flock without the flock losing its autonomy. In order for leaders to represent the autonomous group, the whole group must be given oportunity to vote for or against their appointment. Yes, vote! As selection is usually done, the only voice the people have is to black-ball men after they have been nominated. To object to a man whom the elders nominate is to question their judgment; so the individual voice is usually silenced by intimidation. To exercise this negative vote of objecting can only create strained feelings between the nominee, the objector, and others in the church. A secret ballot would be much more positive, honest, and representative of the people.

"If elders are selected by popular vote, it would be a political race," you may object. Do you deny that church politics and power struggles are involved in our old methods? "It would become a popularity contest and unqualified men would be chosen!" Do you mean that the congregation is unable to judge and that an elite group must limit the choices by selecting the nominees? And what is wrong about an elder being popular? I take no pleasure in asserting that many of the elders that I have known would not have gotten a majority vote of the church. How can one be an effective leader if he is disliked by a majority of those whom he seeks to lead? A man who will not agree to majority vote approval is jealous of his position and has the spirit of lordship.

When the existing eldership restricts the church to its own nominations, the group has lost its freedom to a self-perpetuating body of bishops. The selection becomes as free as a Russian election!

The Scriptures set no tenure for elders, so the length of term of the appointment is left to our judgment. By electing for a specified tenure of years, recall can be made simply by failure of reelection. In our present system, an elder can be recalled only by creating a big, unpleasant scene in the church.

The elders are to be pastors of the flock rather than a board of directors administering from a meeting room. Let the elders be involved chiefly in the spiritual care of the members. Business of the congregation can be carried on by selected servants, committees, and the whole congregation. All business should be done with the general approval of the church. It is admitted that clear distinctions cannot always be made between the spiritual feeding and the business of the church. However, neither the elders nor any other group within the church has the right to obligate the congregation to an expenditure of money, time, or work without consulting the people for their approval. Elders often initiate such programs without consent and then expect cooperation, and wonder at the lack of enthusiasm by those whom they laid the burden on. It is not the load that is burdensome so much as the loss of their freedom to choose.

Who is to have the determining voice in the congregation? If we feel that we must establish an authority structure among disciples, we have at least these four alternatives to choose from or to integrate together:

1. Some situations indicate that the church as a whole made its decisions (Acts 6:1-6; 11:29f; 15:1-4; 15:22, 30-32, 33, 35).

2. We are to submit to our leaders, which leaders are not identified as elders (Heb. 13:7; 1 Cor. 16:15f; 1 Thes. 5:12f).

3. These references indicate that evangelists are given final authority (1 Tim. 4:11; 5:20; 2 Tim. 4:1f; Titus 1:5; 1 Thes. 5:12f; Heb. 13-17; Eph. 4:11f).

4. Some accept the elders as authoritative decision makers (Acts 20:28; 1 Tim. 3:4f; 5:17; Eph. 4:11f; Heb. 13:17).

It seems evident that neither of these four alternatives is established as an exclusive authoritative voice in the congregation. The different circumstances within the various groups would allow for much flexibility to meet their specific needs as long as they respect the priesthood of each believer. Whether one form is accepted or a blending of the four, none will be effective unless disciples are mutually submissive to each other in love (Eph. 5:21; 1 Peter 5:5).

You should have no earthly spiritual rulers for none stand between you and God. Being a priest serving through your High Priest, you need to gain permission from no one to serve and worship according to your understanding of God's will. You are free to leave one congregation in favor of another, or to start a new congregation.

God could have established an authority structure for the churches in one sentence in the epistles, but He didn't. Yet we continue to try to establish a system of authority to be a part of a necessary pattern of organization. Why should we not become wise enough to accept the wisdom of God and to recognize the flexibility that He put in the church to make it adaptable to local circumstances? This flexibility can be maintained only in autonomous congregations where there is a spirit of unity and loyalty.

Chapter 24

THE FREE-FLOWING STREAM

Although it may meander and eddy, a stream seeks the median course. Although it receives pollutants constantly, the flowing stream tends to purify itself. Dam it up and it stagnates and breeds all sorts of scum and slime. The free-flowing stream is in a constant purifying process even though it is never pure in the strictest sense.

So it is with the church. The free, autonomous disciples must be permitted to go unrestricted by earthly rulers. Free people may vary in interpretation and understanding in different congregations and in different generations. The church will have constant danger of impurities, so it will always be in a state of reformation, but, because it is composed of erring humans, it will never be without flaw entirely. One generation cannot crystallize and credalize a system in order to guarantee that its concepts will be bound on the next generation to insure its faithfulness. Efforts to control the next generation are attempts to force unity. When the stream is damned up, it becomes stagnant and will begin to depend upon intellectual inbreeding, which produces doctrinal monstrosities.

Control can come through well-meaning men who have innocent purposes. In the early centuries, the bishops recognized the ignorance and vulnerability of many of the disciples, so they began to explain rules of right and wrong to the flock. They sought to identify final, absolute orthodoxy and demanded conformity to avoid heresy. Thinking to safeguard the ignorant, they built interpretative fences around the law. Thus they began to dam up the stream by their rules. These elders/bishops became the spiritually elite who felt qualified to make their interpretations into binding requirements. Then it became unnecessary for a person to know the scriptures. Why bother to learn scriptures when one must depend upon the bishop for instruction and interpretation anyway? Surely enough, it developed to the logical conclusion that a person was ultimately forbidden to interpret the Bible for himself. If he interpreted it differently from the bishops, he sinned, for they were the authoritative voice and rulers. So it became a sin to read the Bible! All this developed from such good motives!

Misunderstood teachings did not bring apostasy, but bishop power did, damning up the stream. And what a stagnation developed! Its slimy and monstrous concepts have polluted every disciple on earth since that time. Although cracks have been forced in the dam by reformers, the stream is never purified entirely of its gross influences.

That is why I wince inwardly when I hear of elders making rules for God's people today. It is not that I do not love and respect elders. When they set dress codes, specify which version of the Bible one may use, legislate concerning how many assemblies one must attend, tell a person what he must believe to stay in their fellowship, etc., they are seeking to protect and strengthen the flock, but these are steps in the direction of becoming the elite interpreters, controllers, and rulers. So the unholy process begins again. Others may submit to lords, but "it shall not be so among you!" (Matt. 20:26).

Let the saints in each fellowship be free to do their own interpreting and let them be free from the unholy luxury of judging one another. They may veer to the left or right but will constantly be correcting their course through their own desire to follow the truth. If they have not that desire, no rulers or creeds or dams will hold them in the truth anyway. An elite class of rulers ultimately ensalves. Let each fellowship of saints be a free-flowing, self-purifing stream.

Let us be FREE IN CHRIST —
.. free to proclaim Christ as our only creed.
.. free from efforts of legal justification
.. free to accept the grace that is freely given
.. free from condemnation through faith in Christ
.. free to love everyone, thus fulfilling all law
.. free to interpret the scriptures honestly
.. free from interpreting Christ's law as a legal code

.. free from duty and quota performance
.. free to exercise our Christian liberties
.. free from binding our scruples on others
.. free to love and accept without judging
.. free from exclusiveness
.. free to unite in Christ rather than by doctrinal
      conformity
.. free from a distinguishing name, or a need for one
.. free to offer full-life service as a continuous worship
.. free from confidence in keeping legal details and holy
      rituals
.. free to offer spontaneous, undemanded, overflowing
      worship
.. free to commune with all disciples
.. free from men who would be our spiritual rulers
.. free to serve in autonomous fellowships
.. free to re-evaluate all things
.. free to be disciples truly — learning, growing, maturing,
      reforming

Jesus died to give us this cherished freedom. "So if the Son makes you free, you will be free indeed" (John 8:36). So be it!

Chapter 25

WHAT GOD REQUIRES

There is endless Bible study and discussion in a sincere effort to learn what God requires of us. Often, good people are greatly discouraged by the complicated burden which they think that God has laid on them. God's demands seem so involved and vague that the shadow of doubt and insecurity hovers over many a devout disciple because he feels that he might not be understanding what God requires of him. He feels entrapped by the intricate will of his Father.

Because I was born of, and nurtured on, legalism, I shared those feelings for many years. Now, I am beginning to understand that it is we, not the Lord, who have made God's requirements complicated. As the Pharisees complicated the Law of Moses and missed its purposes, so we have sought to define details through which we think to attain our righteousness, and we have made holy details the center of our religion. With such a background, it has been difficult for me to comprehend that "my yoke is easy and my burden is light," that "his commandments are not grievous/burdensome," and that God can make us to stand in spite of our lack of conformity.

God's timeless law is not a complicated system. From Cain and Abel on down to us, God's law has always been: love/respect God, and love/respect man. In various ages and circumstances God has given statutes, laws, ordinances, and regulations to guide the lawless into the practice of this universal law. These stipulations were given because man disregarded the law written in the heart; thus, ". . . the law is not laid down for the just but for the lawless and disobedient, for the ungodly and sinners . . . " (1 Tim. 1:8). But man everywhere has always had the timeless law in his conscience to guide him.

Murder, theft, greed, adultery, and idolatry are not wrong because they are parts of the Ten Commandments or of Jesus' prohibition of those things. They have always been, and always will be, wrong. They are included in the Ten Commandments and in Jesus' teachings because they were wrong already, involving violation of love of God and man.

When God has given ordinances, regulations, and rituals to guide the lawless, man's tendency has been to seek justification in keeping the jot and tittle of the requirement and ritual instead of being guided into expression of love. Such brought Jesus' denunciation of the Pharisees in Matthew 23. Those woes pronounced on them should serve as warnings to us also.

Micah sought to put his people back on the uncomplicated track with this summary of God's universal requirements: "He has showed you, O man, what is good; and what does the Lord require of you but to do justice, and to love kindness, and to walk humbly with your God?" (Micah 6:8). All other ordinances and regulations were but an elaboration of this epitome of all law.

Jesus' covenant was new, but His law was not. He repeated and emphasized God's requirement to love God and man. He concluded by adding, "On these two commandments depend all the law and the prophets" (Matt. 22:40). They were the embodiment of all of God's message to man!

Jesus also summarized all moral law in the Golden Rule, "for this is the law and the prophets" (Matt. 7:12). Paul assures us that all law is summed up and fulfilled in one word — love (Rom. 13:8-10; Gal. 5:14).

The will of God is for love to rule our conduct. Jesus warned, "Not everyone who says to me, 'Lord, Lord,' shall enter the kingdom of heaven, but he who does the will of my Father who is in heaven" (Matt. 7:21). Then He declared that such things as instructing in religion, sensational religious activities, and mighty Christian works were not necessarily the doing of His will.

Cain knew he had sinned because he knew the embodiment of all law relating to God and man. Micah and Jesus, in later ages, gave us similar nut-shell abridgements of all law.

Are these abridgements dangerous because they leave out rituals? We will not suspect the Holy Spirit of being mistaken or indiscreet. There is no sacramental value in rituals. The value imparted to the disciple from rituals and services is the strength he gains from learning and spiritual exercise. He is not justified by them, nor are they measures of his righteousness. They are of value as they encourage the disciple to fulfill the timeless law of love for God and man. They are not what God requires of us, but they are a means to an end, to help us to do His eternal will to love.

Think of all the hair-splitting requirements we have defined concerning the Lord's Supper, for instance, lest we miss its sacramental value or displease a demanding God. In the process, we have alienated people, preventing their communing together. Such misses God's requirement completely!

What does God require? We have often used the thrilling story of the conversion of the Ethiopian eunuch to illustrate the simplicity of the process in becoming a disciple. Now, let us use that story to illustrate the simplicity in meeting God's requirements as a disciple.

Ethiopian Converted

The conversion of the eunuch makes a beautiful story, but have you thought about the final, unwritten chapter of that story? We last see the new convert headed back toward Ethiopia rejoicing in his new faith. But there he will be alone in his faith in Jesus. There is no church to meet with there for the gospel is not yet preached among the Gentiles. So, he will have to "forsake the assembly" before he assembles the first time. He cannot go to worship because there is no worship service of the church. He cannot be taught and edified because there is no gospel preacher in his whole country.

Philip had only preached/evangelized to him Jesus. He did not instruct him in the Apostles' doctrine/teaching. There is a significant difference in preaching and teaching/instructing. A course of instruction was not a prerequisite of conversion, and there is no example of that sort of indoctrination being given in the process of converting anyone. So, here is a lonely disciple who doesn't even know the "five acts of worship," the nature and work of the church, and all the rules and regulations relating to being a Christian. In fact, he doesn't even know about being a Christian because no one had ever used that designation at that time. This poor treasurer doesn't have a copy of the New Testament Scriptures, either, because none were in existence. He does have a copy of Isaiah and, hopefully, some of the other Old Testament Scriptures. He has the teachings of the law and the prophets written in his heart which have sustained his faith as a practicing Jew in Ethiopia.

It would seem that the Holy Spirit used poor judgment in calling Philip from a busy, successful campaign in Samaria down to the Gaza highway just to make one green convert and then let him go immediately to the spiritual wasteland of Ethiopia to wither and die. What a waste of effort! The Spirit caught up Philip when they emerged from the water, and there was no more communication. The eunuch was left on the bank wet. How unmerciful it was that such a receptive and happy man would be allowed to ride off into disappointment and eternal loss.

Surely, it is I who is in judgmental error rather than the Spirit. The Spirit knew what He was doing, and He was not laboring under all my accumulated misunderstandings and misinterpretations.

The Ethiopian Disciple

What will God require of that noble saint in his remote land? He will want him to continue to believe in Jesus and to grow in that faith. His Old Testament Scriptures will serve that need, even as they served other disciples then and now. His copy of Isaiah will have new and reassuring meanings to him now each time he reads it. He will see a picture of his Savior now as he meditates on the rituals of the law. But what about attendance to worship services? Participation in assemblies is not a requirement for justification, but it is intended to be for edification. All should involve themselves in strength building activities. But assemblies are not the only means for keeping faith strong. Many disciples maintain strong faith who have been unable to attend services for years. The eunuch had kept his faith in God strong enough, without such "acts of worship" in assemblies, to cause him to return to Jerusalem for Jewish worship. He had gained his strength from the available Scriptures. Can they not still serve that disciple's purpose well?

How will this displaced brother know what to do in serving God? He can remember that his Scriptures tell him to continue loving God and man. That's what Jesus would stress. Nothing new there. Being a devout Jew, he will surely remember, "He has showed you, O man, what is good; and what does the Lord require of you but to do justice, and to love kindness, and to walk humbly with your God?" (Micah 6:8). Jesus would have him to follow the Golden Rule, "for this is the law and the prophets." James would tell him, "Religion that is pure and undefiled before God and the Father is this: to visit the orphans and widows in their affliction, and to keep oneself unstained from the world." (James 1:27). Jesus and James were only restating God's universal will which the law and the prophets sought to promote. God still wants the same response from man. A man need not have New Testament writings to know the will of God for holy living. Spirit-filled men elaborate on these simple requirements in the epistles, giving practical application among various peoples, cultures, and settings. The treasurer can continue to be a devout disciple in the same general manner that he was a devout Jew.

Too many of us have considered assemblies and their rituals as the major requirement of God and the evident demonstration of our righteousness. But how misdirected we have been! These assemblies and rituals are important only as they strengthen our faith and encourage us to live the kind of daily lives epitomized in the paragraph above. Splitting hairs about how to perform acceptable rituals and chalking up records of frequency of performance of them have little connection with what God requires of us. The eunuch will "go to worship" no more as he did on his long journey to Jerusalem but, instead, his daily life will be a living sacrifice/offering/worship.

"But he will continue his Jewish rituals," you may protest. What's the problem with that? The Judean disciples and Paul did that also (Acts 15; 18:18; 21:17-26). There is no conflict, for they performed neither those Jewish rituals nor Christian rituals in an effort to justify themselves.

Hopefully, the treasurer will influence his family and friends so that they will accept Christ. Then in their discipleship, together, they will engage in such activities as will strengthen their faith and encourage them in fulfilling God's timeless law in their lives. New Testament Scriptures will not be necessary as they continue to call on their God in Christ. But they will look to no activities of theirs for any sacramental or meritorious value and look upon no pattern of conformity as sacred. Each will serve in his individual relationship with God. Collectively, they will be Christ's church, free from all of our theological conceptions and misconceptions about it.

All of this seems too simple to be true, yet I am not going to accuse the Spirit of poor judgment just because I have been confused. Effort was not lost in converting the Secretary of the Treasury of Ethiopia. And if the Spirit's way will suffice for the Ethiopian nobleman, surely it will suffice for you and me.

Being free in Christ, let us, like the eunuch, go on our way rejoicing.